LITERARY/CULTURAL THEORY

FEMINISMS

Literary/Cultural Theory provides concise and lucid introductions to a range of key concepts and theorists in contemporary literary and cultural theory. Original and contemporary in presentation, and eschewing jargon, each book in the series presents students of humanities and social sciences exhaustive overviews of theories and theorists, while also introducing them to the mechanics of reading literary/cultural texts using critical tools. Each book also carries glossaries of key terms and ideas, and pointers for further reading and research. Written by scholar-teachers who have taught critical theory for years, and vetted by some of the foremost experts in the field, the series Literary/Cultural Theory is indispensable to students and teachers.

Series Editors

Allen Hibbard
Middle Tennessee State University

Andrew Slade
University of Dayton

Herman Rapaport
Wake Forest University

Imre Szeman
University of Alberta

Krishna Sen
University of Calcutta

Scott Slovic
University of Idaho

Sumit Chakrabarti
Presidency University, Kolkata

Also in the series

Psychoanalytic Theory and Criticism
Marxist Literary and Cultural Theory
Ecocriticism
Jacques Lacan
New Historicism
Dalit Literature and Criticism
Diaspora Studies
Masculinities
Queer Studies

LITERARY/CULTURAL THEORY

FEMINISMS

ARPITA MUKHOPADHYAY
University of Burdwan

Edited by
SUMIT CHAKRABARTI
Presidency University, Kolkata

Orient BlackSwan

FEMINISMS

ORIENT BLACKSWAN PRIVATE LIMITED

Registered Office
3-6-752 Himayatnagar, Hyderabad 500 029, Telangana, India
e-mail: centraloffice@orientblackswan.com

Other Offices
Bengaluru, Bhopal, Chennai, Ernakulam, Guwahati, Hyderabad, Jaipur, Kolkata, Lucknow, Mumbai, New Delhi, Noida, Patna, Vijayawada

© Orient Blackswan Private Limited 2016
First published 2016
Reprinted 2018

ISBN 978 81 250 6073 4

Typeset in Aldine 401 BT 10.5/13 *by*
Mindshine Book House
Hyderabad 500 060

Printed at
Graphica Printers
Hyderabad 500 013

Published by
Orient Blackswan Private Limited
3-6-752 Himayatnagar, Hyderabad 500 029
e-mail: info@orientblackswan.com

Contents

Editor's Preface	*vii*
Introduction	1
1. Early Feminists	13
2. Simone de Beauvoir and Radical Feminism	30
3. Cultural Feminism and Gynocriticism	44
4. Marxist and Socialist Feminism	51
5. Postmodern Feminism	60
6. *L'écriture Féminine*	68
7. Black Feminism	81
8. Postcolonial Feminism and Third World Feminism	90
9. Ecofeminism	106
10. Lesbian Feminism	111
11. Feminist Criticism in Practice	116
Glossary of Select Terms	127
Suggested Reading	139

Editor's Preface

This volume on feminism, the first in the series under my editorship, attempts the dual manoeuvre of locating feminism/s within both historical and critical perspectives. While it traces the trajectory of women's studies or critical/theoretical treatises on and by women within a teleological frame, it also suitably marks the interventionist criticality that has been a part of the politics of feminism since its inception. The inflective nature of feminism, its dialogic import, has also been keenly addressed in the attempt that this volume makes in noticing the continuous and fraught engagement of feminism with various forms of critical thinking or theoretical frameworks across history.

Agency is that crucial consideration around which the volume has modelled itself. What constitutes agency in feminism? Does feminism have a viable agency at all? How valid or validated (if at all) is that agency, within the various markers of critical theory, on the one hand, and the woman 'living' in society as such, on the other? Is there a possible feminism for all women on this planet? In this context, the book tries to comprehend the 'woman question' in terms of radical interventions, leftisms, race, ecology, sexual preference, culturality, and the differently evolved registers of modernisms and/or postmodernisms within synchronic historical parameters. Through a historico-cultural mapping of the myriad representational tendencies of feminism, the author tries to understand the politics behind the collusive intentions of feminism. Is the 'woman question' a substantive one? Are there possible proto-feminisms lurking behind its agential claims? Does feminism successfully grapple with essentialist tendencies both within and without its theoretical framework?

It is important to address the questions that the volume has raised. However, it is not always possible to elicit easy answers. As the author herself insists in her introduction, feminism needs to be understood in the plural. Exploring and identifying 'feminisms' is the imperative. In a late-capitalist world – sexist and patriarchal, more often than not divided into the easy binaries of 'North' and 'South' – what is most crucial is to register each (im)possible, (in)significant intervention. Even as I write this preface, Malala Yousafzai's Nobel speech about the girl's right to education is overwhelmed by the incident of the Uber-cab rape in New Delhi. How does feminism encounter the woman's fight against the corporation? Or, does it at all?

The volume provides a broad framework within which to locate the possible politics of feminism. The trajectory of feminism, from a movement for the rights of women towards the possibility of an 'organic revolution', has been traced in the volume. The book suitably reiterates what needs to be reiterated continuously: that for women, every moment is political; that myriad forms of essentialisms lurk at every possibility of women assuming a non-political stance; that discourses strategically and necessarily subsume and obliterate the 'woman question'; that both the epistemic and the doxic need to be reframed at every moment of enunciation; that meaning must always be contingent.

For the uninitiated, this volume could be a good handbook. For the professional practitioner, or the academic, it could be a primer for rethinking.

Sumit Chakrabarti

Introduction

Feminism is not a singular or unitary concept, but a polyvalent amalgam of diverse, multi-layered, complex, and often, contradictory ideas. There are various approaches to the issue of feminism, which makes it difficult to arrive upon any single definition. Lisa S. Price, in *Feminist Frameworks: Building Theory on Violence against Women*, offers an interesting definition of the term: 'Feminism is also a method of analysis, a standpoint, a way of looking at the world from the perspective of women. It questions government policies, popular culture, ways of doing and being, and asks how women's lives are affected by these ideological and institutional practices' (6). It must be acceded, from the onset, that feminism needs to be understood in the plural; exploring and identifying 'feminisms' is therefore a more authentic approach. Feminisms address the issue of women's inferior position in society and seek ways and methods of alleviating the social, cultural, political and economic discriminations that women are subjected to. But the differences in the approach to this central problem contribute to the complexity, diversity, fragmentation and contradictions underlying 'feminisms'.

The origin of the term 'feminism' is uncertain and debatable. The term can be traced back to 1871, when it was used as a medical term to define symptoms of 'feminisation' of the bodies of male patients. In 1872, Alexandre Dumas used it in a pamphlet titled *l'homme femme*, to identify women who behaved in a masculine way. And the term had spread through Europe and America by 1910. Thus, 'feminism' as a term had conflicting implications in both medical and political discourse.

The term is made up of two components – 'femme', 'woman' in French, and '-esme', which refers to a social movement or a political ideology. It has been a controversial term and many activists struggling against sexist oppression have even rejected the label. Women fighting for better wages and job security could not always identify themselves with the middle-class, educated, suffragist feminists, while the middle-class women were apprehensive of its radical implications. The earliest use of the term 'feminism' held negative connotations. Margaret Walters, in *Feminism: A Very Short Introduction*, refers to Virginia Woolf's reservations about the term 'feminism', which she expressed in *Three Guineas* (1938). Woolf dismisses it as 'an old word, a vicious and corrupt word that has done much harm in its day' (qtd. in Walters 2). It is interesting to note that 'feminism' as a qualifier was initially not used by women struggling for their rights, even though women's rights movements had started to emerge in the United States with the Seneca Falls Convention of 1848 and the subsequent 'Declaration of Sentiments'. This movement demanded equality for women as citizens, as an implication of the 'Rights of Citizen' ensured in the American 'Declaration of Independence'. But the awareness of the discrimination against women and women activists' attempts to protest/challenge these discriminatory practices had emerged even before the suffrage movement in the United States and England. Mary Wollstonecraft (1759–97) had published her influential *A Vindication of the Rights of Women* in 1792, while women such as Olympe de Gouges (1748–93) in France were voicing the necessity of conferring political and economic rights, similar to those accorded to men, to women. Hence, the origins of feminism as a movement are diverse, depending on specific oppressive practices across time and space. While women have offered resistance against exploitative practices for centuries, feminism as a concerted political movement containing several tendencies is a twentieth century phenomenon.

In order to classify the shifting movements in the history of feminism, the paradigm of 'waves' came into use. Thus, 'first wave feminism' is used to signify the feminist movements of the late-nineteenth century and the early-twentieth century that were aimed at acquiring equal rights for women. 'Second wave feminism' refers to the feminist movements of the 1960s and 70s that addressed issues such as women's employment, role in the family and sexuality, along with their political rights. However, the practice of using 'waves' to classify historical moments in the feminist movement runs the risk of implying that there was no feminist activity outside the scope of these umbrella terms. The fact remains that there were numerous political, cultural and social movements which cannot be contained within these neat divisions. Rather, the heterogeneity of the theories and actions related to feminist issues run beyond the convenient compartments intended to understand the development of feminist thought. Apart from the historical approach, attempts are also made to group feminist activity and attitudes under different theoretical frameworks. Broadly, they are put under three categories: Liberal feminism, Marxist or Socialist feminism and Radical feminism. Liberal feminism argues for equal rights for women based on the ideology of the liberal state of equal rights and privileges for all citizens. Marxist or Socialist feminist system believes that gender inequality is related to the capitalist mode of production, while Radical feminists identify patriarchy to be the root of all evils against women. Apart from these broad categories, there are several other categories such as psychoanalytic feminism, postmodern feminism, black feminism, postcolonial feminism, poststructural feminism, cyberfeminism and so on.

The first wave of feminist movement was simply 'the woman's movement'. The movement comprised struggle for legal and political rights. The suffragists, however, did not override the idea that motherhood wielded social and domestic authority. After 1910, a younger generation of activists articulated a marked preference for a 'feminist' political identity, advocating equal rights, often rejecting the maternal paradigm. The earlier feminists were concerned with the 'right to earn their living', but with time, feminism acquired varied connotations across different parts of the world depending on the heterogeneity of experiences. Since its origin, till its wider circulation in the 1960s, the feminist label had a pejorative undertone. Universal adult suffrage was extended to women in England and other countries between 1928 and the 1940s, but there was an ongoing debate about the comparative merit of the terms 'humanist' and 'feminist' vis-à-vis the women's movement. Liberal feminism advocates women's equality in professional, political and public life. They argue that society's discriminatory attitude towards women is solely predicated on the assumption that they are the 'weaker sex'. This impedes women from exercising free choice. Liberal feminists do not reject the capitalist system of production, since they believe this system will provide them with opportunities of realising their potentials.

Liberal feminism starts with Mary Wollstonecraft's *A Vindication of the Rights of Women*, John Stuart Mill's (1806–73) *Subjection of Women* (1869) and the Women's Suffrage Movement in both the United Kingdom and the United States. Liberal feminists found discrimination against women in the public sphere – in society's denial of giving them access to education, politics, financial independence and general intellectual life. Men wielded power and authority in the Church, in the state and within families. Women had no legal or political rights and had restricted access to higher education. Queen Elizabeth ascended the throne of England in 1558 and reigned successfully over a long period of time. Subsequent political events, such as the English Civil War and the Glorious Revolution of 1688, destabilised the sovereignty of the monarch. There were also perceived tentative attempts at challenging patriarchal rule. Some subversive texts challenging the Genesis myth were in circulation, such as Jane Anger's *Her Protection for Women* (1589) and Rachel Speght's *A Mouzell for Melastomus* (1617). Working-class women often protested against legislative and social discriminations. Writers such as Aphra Behn (1640–89) and Lady Chudleigh (1656–1710) were articulating their views on the subordination of women at the hands of men. The Quakers played a crucial role in inculcating awareness against discriminatory practices based on gender and race. In an ideal Quaker family, men and women enjoyed equality of status, which was reflected in the fact that 'Quaker women comprised 40 per cent of female abolitionists, 19 per cent of feminists born before 1830, and 15 per cent of suffragists born before 1830' (Mary Maples, qtd. in Jenainati and Groves 13).

During the eighteenth and nineteenth centuries, several thinkers and social reformers debated in favour of women's claims to social and political equality. The legacy of the Enlightenment, the emphasis on rationality instead of faith, and the increasing importance of free inquiry resulted in challenges to the status quo. This included arguments and polemics about the subordinate position of women in society. John Stuart Mill, Mary Wollstonecraft and Harriet Martineau (1802–76) provided the intellectual impetus for this first wave of feminism. These first-wave feminists struggled against inequalities in opportunities of education, employment and political rights, and unjust marriage laws. Wollstonecraft challenged the assumptions of Rousseau in *A Vindication of the Rights of Women*, advocating equal participation of women in public life and greater empowerment in economic and private spheres. Her insistence on sexual equality and her radical views on marriage were not well received in her time. This was largely due to the unconventionality of her personal life, revealed in the *Memoirs* authored by her husband, William Godwin. Social reformers John Stuart Mill and Harriet Taylor Mill (1807–58) debated the 'woman question', gender roles, inequality and subordination of women in essays such as *On Subjection of Women* (1869) and *The Enfranchisement of Women* (1851). Though their views occasionally hinted at certain prevalent prejudices about motherhood and domesticity, they were largely supportive of social transformation that accommodated the rights and dignity of women.

In the turbulence of the 1960s, women's movements gained momentum under the banner of 'women's liberation', which soon was derisively abridged as 'women's libbers'. The 60s offers an interesting area of investigation. During the Second World War, women were compelled to join the workforce but by the end of the war, women were expected to return to the 'homes' – domesticity was emphasised, as was women's role as nurturers and care-givers, the agencies of socialisation; and consumerism became significant. Women were also present in the workforce in significant numbers, which was at odds with the idealisation of the nuclear family unit. As a result, feminism in the 60s acquired a diversity of perspectives depending on race and class positions. Feminist movements in the 60s were also influenced by, and overlapped with, other political, social and cultural movements like the students' movements in Europe and America, the Civil Rights Movement and the anti-Vietnam War movements. The second wave was, however, far-reaching with women not only demanding political and legal equality but also control over their reproductive and sexual roles. Another significant paradigm shift was discerned after the 1960s – feminist movement championed not just demands for equality but also insisted upon the acknowledgement of the 'difference' between men and women. This coincided with the ascendant use of the term 'gender', instead of 'sex', underscoring the importance of the social 'constructedness' of the idea of the 'feminine', and not just biology determining the paradigms of masculinity and femininity. As a term, 'feminism' did not enjoy wide popularity, but it signified, with moderate success, certain political, social and cultural goals. This is largely due to the fact that feminism, as a concept, has continuously modified itself to address varied concerns, stake-holders and debates. Thus, over the last decades of the twentieth century, feminism was appended to qualifiers to produce new compounds, all addressing the diversity of its praxis – black feminism, Asian-American feminism, postcolonial feminism, lesbian feminism, ecofeminism and Islamic feminism attest to the complexity of this label.

Radical feminists, however, do not agree with Liberal feminists on the resolution of the discrimination against women. According to the former, change in political and legal structures ensuring greater empowerment for women can address the problem only partially; the structures of oppression are so deeply entrenched in patriarchy that only a complete overhaul of social, political and personal ideology can bring about meaningful change in women's condition. Radical feminism, in all its various approaches, explores the reproductive and sexual roles of women. Androgyny was upheld as an ideal mode of experience for both men and women by some Radical feminists. A few others, however, scoffed at the idea of androgyny. They debated the over-emphasis on distinguishing 'masculine' and 'feminine' traits. Radical feminism also underlines the importance of flexibility in exercising sexuality by women. However, the Radical-Cultural feminist theorists emphasise celibacy, autoeroticism, and even lesbianism as exclusive expressions of female sexuality, since pornography, rape, ritualistic genital mutilation, *sati* and *purdah* are instances of degradation of women based on dominant male sexuality. Regarding motherhood, there is a stark divide in attitudes between the Radical-Libertarian and the Radical-Cultural feminists. While the former group advocates absolute freedom of choice vis-à-vis motherhood, the Cultural feminists celebrate and valorise motherhood as a unique and empowering experience for women.

Marxist and Socialist feminists insisted that women's oppression is a result of capitalism. In a deeply classist society, patriarchy is inevitable. To instil gender equality, both patriarchy and capitalism should be dismantled. Socialist feminism sought to assimilate several forms of women's oppression in order to underline the layered and complex ways of subordination inflicted upon women. Other Socialist feminists such as Iris Marion Young (1949–2006) and Heidi Hartmann (b.1945) did not single out patriarchy or capitalism as determining factors of women's oppression, but hinted at an interface between the two causing the devaluation of women in both the public and the private spheres.

Psychoanalytical feminists turned their enquiry inwards; unlike Liberal, Radical, Marxist or Socialist feminists, they tried to analyse the forms and structures of oppression as internalised and expressed in the psyche. Psychoanalysts sought to understand the psychosexual implications of the paradigms of 'masculinity' and 'femininity'. Theorists such as Julia Kristeva (b.1941), Hélène Cixous (b.1937) and Luce Irigaray (b.1930) concerned themselves with the pre-Oedipal, pre-linguistic stage of experience. Lacanian psychoanalysis distinguishes this stage as the 'imaginary' stage from the 'symbolic' stage which signals the entry of the infant into the linguistic/civilising/patriarchal domain. The French psychoanalytic feminists explore the creative, instinctual aspects of the imaginary stage along with underlining the affirmative, liberatory aspect of the mother-child dyad, hitherto held as restrictive in Freudian psychoanalysis. Thinkers such as Carol Gilligan (b.1936), Nel Noddings (b.1926) and Sara Ruddick (1935–2011) examine the differences between the 'masculine' and the 'feminine' and offer their hypothesis of the 'ethics of care' and the 'ethics of justice'. In this scheme of things, women are attributed with greater capacity for care, while men are driven by rationality and intellect.

Postcolonial, multicultural feminism seeks to identify the differences that exist between women. They subvert the monistic myth of the category 'woman', underlining the varieties of female experience across caste, class, race and sexuality. This diversification of feminism challenges essentialism and chauvinism by emphasising the contexts of women's oppression. The differences in age, religion, education, occupation, health, domestic status, etc., contribute to the plurality of women's material reality.

The third wave of feminism and postmodern feminism attack the binaries of the 'masculine' and the 'feminine', 'sex' and 'gender', inherent in patriarchal structures. The third-wave feminists assert the importance of difference in speaking, thinking and writing for and about women. It is increasingly a challenge for contemporary feminists to merge the inevitability of the contradictions in women's experiences and the necessity of finding shared dimensions and commonality in these experiences. This makes us question whether the possibility of a global sisterhood is a reality or a myth. Again, the validity and authenticity of such a sisterhood can also be put to test.

In the 1980s, the idea of 'postfeminism' started gaining ground. It is diverse in its implications. The prefix 'post' led to a number of analyses of the phenomenon. To some, it implied a movement beyond sexism and feminism, while to others, it meant feminism's obsolescence altogether. A significant aspect of postfeminism is its marked departure from any social agenda. Postfeminism is, on another level, connected to anti-feminist attitude, not just restricted to the twentieth century; it is present whenever feminism poses a threat to the patriarchal status quo. In this respect, 'postfeminism' as a concept is ambiguous. It subsumes the contradictory discourses of discouraging women from pursuing their own interests and bemoaning the inequality of status inflicted on them. The equality-difference dialectic is, in this case, differently realised. Audrey Bilger states,

> Women are urged to "choose" family over career as though there were no alternative options, to exercise their right to be feminists as though femininity conflicted with political rights,

to celebrate yet again the "year of the woman" as though feminism had reached its peak and one year would compensate for several millennia's worth of the year of the man. (qtd. in Wallace 450)

In the 1990s, the younger generation of women made a decisive and conscious movement beyond the 'second wave'. Rebecca Walker (b.1969), daughter of Alice Walker (b.1944), the African-American writer who famously coined the term 'womanist', prefers the term 'third wave' to 'postfeminism'. The third-wave feminists, significantly, accept the label 'feminist'.

Feminism is now understood as broad-based and not restricted to white, middle-class, educated women. It addresses and encompasses the diversity, differences and contradictions of women's experiences across race, caste, class and sexuality. The definition of feminism put forward by Estelle B. Freedman, in *No Turning Back: The History of Feminism and the Future of Women*, contains the key elements of feminism as a social, cultural, political and personal movement for freedom and equality:

> Feminism is a belief that women and men are inherently of equal worth. Because most societies privilege men as a group, social movements are necessary to achieve equality between women and men, with the understanding that gender always intersects with other social hierarchies. (7)

For many feminists, the contentions within postmodernist, poststructuralist and psychoanalytic criticism are merely academic, since they elide the 'real' experiences of women. It is alleged that these debates are situated within the context of intellectual, affluent, urban women and their limited intellectual circle. Feminism fundamentally entails the struggle against the sexist oppression perpetrated by patriarchy. Women were traditionally discriminated against on essentialist grounds – the qualities of rationality, aggression and leadership were held 'masculine', while, gentleness and intuitiveness were considered 'feminine' traits. These assumptions, compounded by the biological differences among the sexes, resulted in the marginalisation of women. These essentialist assumptions empowered men in both public and private lives and relegated women to an inferior position. The equality-difference issue is central to almost all feminist debates. The debate is whether women should demand equality with men or celebrate their differences from men. But the debate is more problematic and it cannot be understood by such binarisms, since the categories 'equality' and 'differences' are fraught with complications. The major point of contention is, of course, sexual difference, which feminists across different theoretical groups believe to be the issue upon which discrimination has been rife. It has been assumed to be a 'natural' difference between men and women, which has, in its turn, spawned social, political and economic disparities in different cultures and societies. This 'natural' sexual difference between men and women has historically consigned women to a subordinate position, locating her as 'closer to nature', while men have been traditionally assigned a state 'closer to culture'. This determined the roles that women were inscribed in.

Another debate which underlies feminist theory is concerned with the distinction between the categories of 'sex' and 'gender'. The questions that are contingent upon any enquiry directed towards understanding the categories of 'masculinity' and 'femininity' are whether they are qualities which are inherent and biologically determined or whether they are socially constructed. There are Darwinian philosophers, such as Helena Cronin, who argue in favour of 'natural' tendencies/qualities of men and women, where 'men are by nature more ambitious, status-conscious, dedicated, single-minded and persevering than women' (qtd. in Tripp 2). There are feminist theorists who challenge these essentialist assumptions about 'masculinity' and 'femininity'. They argue that ideas about these categories evolve and change with respect to differences in culture and at different historical points. It is only in the latter part of the twentieth century that a distinction was made between 'sex' and 'gender' – that is, the biologically assigned 'maleness' and 'femaleness' and the culturally ascribed set of characteristics termed as 'masculine' and 'feminine'. In 1968, American psychoanalyst Robert Slotter published *Sex and Gender* in which he distinguished between these two terms. Anna Tripp, in *Gender*, points out, 'From the late 1960s onwards, it began to be possible to use the term "gender" to signify all those culturally produced assumptions, expectations, conventions and stereotypes, concerning "appropriate" demeanor and "nomal" behavior for women and for men' (4).

'Feminism' as a term is treated with anxiety and scepticism by women who are younger and beneficiaries of the crusades of the first and second generations of feminists. Feminism is diverse in its implications and hence, it resists generalisation and all attempts towards synoptic analysis. It is inarguably a difficult enterprise to provide a definition and a genealogy of feminism and to trace the development of feminism, considering the complexity, heterogeneity and diversity of the movement. The category 'woman' is accused of overriding the differences among women with respect to race, class, caste, ethnicity and sexuality. With second-wave feminism, white, heterosexual women became the unacknowledged norm, so that they enjoyed a sense of entitlement, a prior claim to feminism as an ideology, resulting in the erasure of racial, sexual, class-based minorities among 'women'. Can inclusions or 'add-ons' be an answer to exclusionist hegemonic hierarchical structures? Can all differences collapse into a 'global sisterhood'? On deeper reviewing, the question is not about the possibility but rather the authenticity of such a synthesis.

Feminism seeks to address the inequalities that exist between men and women in a society. Feminists refuse to accept these disparities as natural and seek to examine the material reality of the lives of women to understand and explain the pedagogy of oppression. Traditionally, the production of knowledge has been androcentric, that is, men have been the producers of knowledge, while women are relegated to the position of being objects inscribed in/by androcentric knowledge. Feminism challenges this status quo, by seeking to produce/generate knowledge about and for women. This project is riddled with a few contradictions regarding the agency and nature of representation. Feminism resists easy formulations and categorisations by virtue of its intersectionality and interdisciplinarity. Any attempt towards putting feminism into neat little categories is doomed to fail, since feminism is *not* monolithic. The various kinds of feminisms – Liberal, Radical, Marxist, postcolonial – signal the variety of approaches and attitudes towards women's oppression. Postmodernism challenges the assumptions of binaries in which gender is constructed, so that the future of feminism is variable, heterogeneous and open-ended. Holly Devor's observation, in *Gender Blending: Confronting the Limits of Duality*, is especially pertinent:

> Members of society might be taught to value adaptability and flexibility rather than the obedience to gender roles, so that the most respected and socially valued personality types would be those which were able to make use of any behaviours which served their purpose in any situation. . . . Men and women, masculinity and femininity, would be seen as immature stages in the process of reaching a blended gender identity and display. (153–54)

REFERENCES

Devor, Holly. *Gender Blending: Confronting the Limits of Duality*. Bloomington: Indiana UP, 1989. Print.

Freedman, Estelle B. *No Turning Back: The History of Feminism and the Future of Women*. New York: Ballantine Books, 2002. Print.

Jenainati, Cathia, and Judy Groves. *Introducing Feminism*. Cambridge: Totem Books, 2007. Print.

Price, Lisa S. *Feminist Frameworks: Building Theory on Violence against Women*. Delhi: Aakar Books, 2009. Print.

Tripp, Anna, ed. *Gender*. London: Palgrave, 2000. Print.

Walters, Margaret. *Feminism: A Very Short Introduction*. Oxford: Oxford UP, 2005. Print.

Wallace, Elizabeth Kowaleski, ed. *Encyclopedia of Feminist Literary Theory*. New York: Routledge, 2009. Print.

Chapter One

Early Feminists

The rise of feminism as an ideology in Europe and America can be traced back to the mid-eighteenth century as a corollary or a consequence of the ideals emerging from the Enlightenment and the French Revolution. The tensions and the conflicts of the historical-philosophical phenomena of the Enlightenment and the French Revolution informed the concurrent debates and deliberations concerning the role and position of women in society. Political upheavals, the tumult of new ideas and economic changes contributed to the development of feminist thought. Contemporary debates about the 'rights of man', and Enlightenment philosophy's emphasis on human nature and rationality significantly influenced eighteenth-century considerations about the 'woman question'. The conceptual grid used to define the relations between the sexes in the eighteenth century was that of the master-slave or despot-subject, based on the assumed physical and intellectual differences between them. Contemporary medical and scientific opinion substantiated the view that these differences were natural or biological rather than social or cultural. Masculinity and femininity were constructed as binaries – the former was assigned rational, objective and scientific properties, while the latter was saddled with the stereotypes of emotionalism, sensuality and irrationality. Thinkers such as Jean Jacques Rousseau (1712–78) reinforced this dichotomy. Rousseau, in *Emile* (1762), propounded different models of education based on sexual difference. He proposed that education for boys should be intended to develop their natural instincts for freedom and autonomy training them to be ideal citizens, while girls should be so educated that they fit the mould of good mother and wife. Socialisation of women was also undertaken by the popular 'conduct books' that recommended feminine virtues of modesty, chastity, piety and meekness.

The appearance of treatises such as Thomas Paine's (1737–1809) *The Rights of Man* (1791), however, raised expectations of inclusion of not only the 'rights of man' but also the 'rights of woman' in the post-Revolutionary society. The early feminists were legatees of the Enlightenment philosophy that privileged the role of rationalism in the formation of a better social order. Education was given primacy in instilling the spirit of free inquiry and liberal ideas. It was believed that the 'rights of woman' and her position in society would be acknowledged if ignorance and corruption could be eradicated through education. These feminist thinkers forcefully challenged the assumptions about female inferiority and offered alternative views on marriage, politics and education. They interrogated the disparity in legal rights and discriminatory practices underlying the institution of marriage, contending in favour of women's rights of citizenship and participation in all aspects of public life. The early feminist thinkers were, as Rossi points out, 'cosmopolitan members of an urban intelligentsia' (5). Feminist philosophers, such as Mary Wollstonecraft (1759–97), Olympia de Gouges (1748–93), Germaine de Stael (1766–1817), Margaret Fuller (1810–50) and Harriet Martineau (1802–76), articulated their convictions and opinions in several polemical texts of the contemporary age. While the English feminist thinkers found equivalence between political oppression and patriarchal oppression, nineteenth-century American feminists, on the other hand, found an analogy between the oppression of women and that of slaves at the hand of their masters. The pioneers of feminist thought, influenced by the Enlightenment philosophy, relied more on the written word and less on activism. However, with the gradual evolution of the feminist movement, activism became an important part, especially in the Women's Suffrage Movement in the United States.

MARY WOLLSTONECRAFT

Mary Wollstonecraft contributed significantly to the debates concerning women's role in politics and society, and in her own way, sought to fight gender inequality. Called 'a Hyena in a petticoat' by none other than Horace Walpole, Wollstonecraft was an exceptional and exemplary figure, consciously transgressing norms in private and public lives. An unconventional woman, a female intellectual and a social pariah, her writings articulate the hope of transforming society to make room for individuals like her. Wollstonecraft's first published work was a collection of polemical essays, *Thoughts on the Education of Daughters*, written in 1787 and largely based on her own experiences. She also wrote a thinly veiled autobiographical novel, *Mary*, and planned *Original Stories*, a collection of children's stories. She was greatly stimulated by the events in France in 1789. Wollstonecraft gave a scathing response to Edmund Burke's *Reflections on the Revolution in France* (1790) in her *A Vindication of the Rights of Men, in a Letter to the Right Honourable Edmund Burke* (1790). With this pamphlet, Wollstonecraft came immediately into the vortex of contemporary political debates. This was followed by *A Vindication of the Rights of Woman* (1792) which firmly established her in the precincts of feminist theory.

A Vindication of the Rights of Woman is a pioneering text in the history of feminist thought. It was intended to be a response to the contemporary debates about women's education and female conduct, specifically to a pamphlet, *Report on Public Instruction*, written by Charles Maurice de Talleyrand-Périgord, a French politician. In this pamphlet, Talleyrand-Périgord proposed a national education policy under the new French constitution. He insisted that French girls be educated with their brothers in public schools till the age of eight and subsequently remain at home and prepare themselves for their domestic roles. This becomes the major point of debate for Wollstonecraft's treatise; she urges Talleyrand-Périgord to revise his plan and not deprive women of their rights. It also needs to be noted that Wollstonecraft had written a review of Catherine Macaulay's *Letters on Education* (1790), in the

Analytic Review, in 1790. Here, she defended Macaulay's argument that contemporary women suffered due to their lack of education and ambivalent social position. The same indignation is also voiced in *A Vindication of the Rights of Woman*; she asserts that there is no fundamental difference between men and women, except for their social environment. Inequality of the sexes can be mitigated by eradicating the discrepancies in their upbringing, emerging from the differences in their education. She argues for equal education and greater access for women to professional opportunities, and denounces the value of 'gallantry' and coquetry in social practices. These, she believes, will ensure the possibility of women fulfilling their central role in the domestic setup in a new social order. She identifies social inequality as the foundation of many social evils; she accommodates gender differences but critiques the predominant social conventions and education that perpetuate the principles of feminine modesty and virtue:

> Strengthen the female mind by enlarging it, and there will be an end to blind obedience, but as blind obedience is ever sought for by power, tyrants and sensualists are in the right when they endeavour to keep women in the dark because the former only want slaves and the latter a play-thing. (34)

She condemns the prevalent state of society, challenging the injustices of property and rank, championing greater equality. Wollstonecraft denounces the vanity of upper-class women who devote their lifetime to pleasing men. She exhorts them to cultivate moral values instead of frittering away their time in acquiring physical beauty. Her treatise particularly addresses middle-class women, who are, in her opinion, uncorrupted by wealth and luxury, not mired in the drudgery of poverty, and thus amenable to rational argument. She insists that femininity is a 'construct', a set of assumptions, ascribed to women and by which they are indoctrinated, thereby forcing them to submit to the oppressive patriarchal order. To challenge this status quo, women need economic independence and access to empowering education. In its insistence on education and autonomy for women, *A Vindication of the Rights of Woman* is fundamentally a political statement.

Wollstonecraft refutes the existence of 'sexual virtues'; she contends that there cannot be virtues that are exclusive to one sex. Thus, 'virtues' that have been traditionally ascribed to women, such as modesty and chastity, can be applied to both the sexes. Wollstonecraft advocates marriage based on egalitarian principles and the revision of marriage laws that would enable and empower women. She also espouses political representation and political roles for women: 'I really think that women ought to have representatives, instead of being arbitrarily governed without any direct share allowed them in the deliberations of government' (155). *A Vindication of the Rights of Woman* is founded on Enlightenment thought in its expressed scepticism for institutions and in its insistence on reason.

JOHN STUART MILL

John Stuart Mill (1806–73), the leading liberal philosopher of the nineteenth century, wrote on a wide range of issues with special emphasis on social and political philosophy. He put forward a progressive theory advocating equality for women in society. The chief hindrances to this were, according to Mill, the social and legal conditions which were severely restrictive to women's freedom. The position of women, especially in marriage, in the nineteenth century, could be compared to slavery. Mill believed that improved conditions for women would ensure that they were no longer victims of abusive husbands but equal partners in a marital relationship. Equality for women would consolidate the creation of family as a model of the 'virtues of freedom'. Mill argued that the subjection of women in society had been due to the assumption of the 'natural' inferiority of women with respect to men.

Mill's *The Subjection of Women* (1869) is an impassioned plea for equality and inclusion of women in social and political life. His liberal and progressive attitude towards the disenfranchised group is manifest in his championing the participation of women in the political arena. Mill states his intention, at the opening of the essay, in no uncertain terms:

> The object of this Essay is to explain as clearly as I am able, the grounds of an opinion which I have held from the very earliest period when I had formed any opinions at all on social or political matters, . . . That the principle which regulates the existing social relations between two sexes – the legal subordination of one sex to the other – is wrong in itself, and now one of the chief hindrances to human improvement. . . . (373)

In the essay, which is a significant feminist polemic, Mill argues that the central problem confronting women is a lack of rational choice. Women are compelled to yield to the servitude of marriage as they are denied autonomy. To be independent, he contends, women need to earn their own livelihood. Women can be, in the true sense, free only when the relations between the sexes are based on equality rather than on the tyranny and domination of men over women. In fact, female subordination, Mill claims, is a detriment to the advancement of both society and the individual. He insists that the subordination of women has been perpetuated based on the belief that they are naturally inferior to men. Mill argues that the 'true' nature of women cannot be determined since it is a result of social conditioning. He acknowledges the importance vested on the institution of marriage in the Victorian era, but points out that the idealisation of home as the 'school of moral cultivation' leads to the stereotyping of woman as a moral exemplar – pure, inviolate and above the sin-ridden material world. Mill finds this glorification of women as 'tiresome cant' which serves only to reinforce the husband's tyranny. Mill insists that the home in reality is 'domestic slavery'; the wife is not the 'angel of the house' but a slave to the despotic husband: 'I am far from pretending that wives are in general no better treated than slaves; but no slave is a slave to the same lengths, and in so full a sense of the word, as a wife is' (394). This imbalance in the domestic structure is anchored in the principle of injustice which then leads to other forms of oppression. Mill emphasises that women have traditionally undergone cultural conditioning to enslave their minds and perpetuate the status quo of the domination-subordination pattern. He advocates equality between the sexes that can only be brought about by fostering equality in education and opportunities. But Mill's idea of the opportunities available to women to ensure equality is fraught with ambiguities as is his understanding of women's nature. After decrying the overemphasis on women's nature as a tool for discrimination, Mill curiously foregrounds women's nature as the necessitating factor in allowing them liberty and equality. Julia Annas's comment is pertinent here: 'The reader is left with the impression that nature has been expelled from the argument as an enemy only to be brought in again by the back door' (63). Similarly, his insistence at the end of chapter 2, that marriage is a valid career for women, citing the principle of the division of labour between men and women, is irreconcilable with his thesis of equality based on women's right to earn their livelihood. Twentieth-century commentators of feminism severely attacked Mill's proposition that a woman has legal claim only to the property that she brings into the marriage and over her own earnings. The arguments disfavouring Mill's thesis can be responded to from the standpoint of the socio-cultural milieu in which he was writing his treatise. Mill's insistence that the 'nature' of men and women are different due to their education and circumstances may seem contradictory to the central argument of the essay, but it presages a major split in twentieth-century feminist theory – between the oppositional concerns of egalitarian and 'difference' feminism. He anticipates the equality-versus-difference debate of twentieth-century feminist movement. His suggestions regarding the legal rights of women over property may seem limiting, but it has to be kept in mind that Mill was arguing in favour of property rights for women at a time when they had none. Mill occupies a significant place in the history of feminism, articulating the concerns and contradictions of the eighteenth and the nineteenth centuries and anticipating the twentieth-century elements in *The Subjection of Woman*.

THE AMERICAN WOMEN'S SUFFRAGE MOVEMENT

Enlightenment feminists such as Wollstonecraft, Fuller and Martineau differed from the later feminists termed as 'moral crusaders' (Rossi 247) on a very important aspect. The Enlightenment feminists were engaged in writing books and delivering lectures on women's rights, but later feminists such as Elizabeth Cady Stanton (1815–1902) and Lucretia Mott (1793–1880) moved from individual intellectual articulation to organised social activism. Wollstonecraft, Wright and Martineau wrote from their personal experiences of discrimination and deprivation as women vis-à-vis economic and professional opportunities; they had to work to achieve their economic security and were aware of the attendant predicaments. Stanton and Mott, on the other hand, did not have the compulsion to earn their livelihood. This, of course, did not hinder their feelings of solidarity towards working women, but they were not as vehement as the Enlightenment feminists in their articulation for changes in the economic and family systems that were deemed to be oppressive to women. Wollstonecraft and Wright were sceptical of religious institutions, while the 'moral crusaders' were fundamentally pious and morally passionate though advocating a more liberal theological framework. The early American feminist movement was deeply imbricated in other social movements of the time. Of them four are crucial: the moral reform (involving the closing down of brothels), the temperance movement (advocating abstinence), the anti-slavery movement and the women's rights movement. The differences between the Enlightenment feminists and their successors are, however, not fundamentally ideological; only their nature of articulation and execution took different forms. As Rossi points out, 'It would, however, be an error to exaggerate these differences between the two groups of feminists, for they shared many traits as well. They were all libertarian, rational, and committed to an enlargement of the aspirations and the opportunities of women' (250).

In 1848, the little country town of Seneca Falls in upstate New York witnessed a number of zealous women and interested men gathering to hold the first meeting in the world devoted entirely to women's rights. In this convention a 'Declaration of Rights and Sentiments' was adopted, which offered certain remarkable propositions. It stated, 'The history of mankind is a history of repeated injuries and usurpations on the part of man toward woman, having in direct object the establishment of an absolute tyranny over her' (Web, n.p.). The idea of womanhood proposed in the 'Declaration' had a polemical power that was lacking in Wollstonecraft's treatise. In the deliberations at the Seneca Fall, the signatories pointed out that women were legally the subjects of husbands and fathers, that wives did not have property rights, and that women were deprived of proper education that would have enabled them to choose professions as doctors and lawyers. Women were excluded from political institutions and deprived of the right to vote. This was reflective of the assumption that women lacked the intellectual ability necessary for political participation. They were expected to create loving homes, raise children and be subordinate to their husbands. What was different in the Seneca Falls Movement was the nascent acknowledgment of the solidarity of women across different classes and races that found greater urgency, strength and application in the next few decades. This was largely due to the encompassment of slavery as a metaphor to define the condition of women. Women engaged in the Abolitionist Movement provided an impetus to the women's rights movement. The coercion and containment of women by their husbands and fathers were likened to the condition of bonded slaves. Their hopes and expectations of universal suffrage after the Civil War were unfortunately belied. The Reconstruction Amendment pointedly excluded women's suffrage by introducing the category 'male' into the Constitution for the first time.

Lucy Stone (1818–93), Elizabeth Cady Stanton and Susan B. Anthony (1820–1906) were leading figures of nineteenth-century women's movement in America. Their predecessors were Lucretia Mott, Abby Kelley (1811–87) and the Grimké sisters – Sarah Moore Grimké (1792–1873) and Angelina Emily Grimké (1805–79) – and they continued the tradition of feminist-Abolitionist activism in post-Civil War suffragism. They were faced with the dilemma of choosing between the Abolitionist and the feminist causes – the 'new woman', such as Anthony and Stone, chose the latter. It should be kept in mind that the Abolitionist and feminist movements in America had a common origin and it was a transition from one to another. Though the three leaders shared the same beliefs about female emancipation and equality between the sexes, their individual struggles present the subtle differences that existed in the broad spectrum of the feminist-Abolitionist movement in nineteenth-century America.

Lucy Stone was an influential figure in the early feminist movement. After graduating from Oberlin College in 1847, she worked as a lecturer for the American Anti-slavery Society. She lectured not only on Abolitionist issues but also on women's issues in different parts of the country, presenting a unique phenomenon of a woman speaking publicly in any capacity. In 1869, Stone along with Julia Ward Howe (1819–1910) and Josephine Ruffin (1842–1924) formed the American Woman Suffrage Association (AWSA) in Boston. She also edited the *Woman's Journal*, a feminist weekly, for over twenty years.

Elizabeth Cady Stanton, unlike Lucy Stone, did not fit into easy categories, because of her bold thinking and radicalism. Like the other 'moral crusaders', she was a passionate Abolitionist as well as a feminist activist. She shared in their belief that emancipation of women would ensure the progress of the human race in general. She adhered to the view that held motherhood as the highest function of women but challenged the assumption that women should be imprisoned in this role. The 1848 'Declaration of Sentiments', which Stanton helped formulate, articulated the collective anger of the group assembled at Seneca Falls at the exclusion of women from suffrage. She detected the social customs and attitudes, reinforced by the Church, that were specifically discriminatory against women. *The Woman's Bible*, a two-part book, was published by Stanton and a 'Revising Committee' of twenty-six women, in 1895 and 1898. It caused a considerable stir by challenging the Church's interpretation of the Bible underscoring their parochialism, hypocrisy and arrogance that deprived women of their dignity and equality. It was occasioned by the intersection of the women's movement and a period of spiritual crisis in America and can be situated in a crucial moment in the history of women's rights movements. The suffragettes in 1848 had expressed their conviction that the interpretation of scriptures was one of the chief obstacles to the emancipation of women from orthodox and corrupt social customs. *The Woman's Bible* is a collection of passages from the Bible which are about women or depicting certain attitudes towards women, followed by commentaries. It is, however, not a systematic theological treatise but an attempt to gain insight into, and reinterpret, the scriptures to establish that the scriptures did not intend women to be placed in a position subservient to men.

Susan B. Anthony was a collaborator, ally and the most intimate friend to Stanton, though their attitudes and approaches were disparate. Like Stanton, Anthony was an ardent suffragist, organiser and speaker at different conventions and lectures and was dedicated to the cause of women's emancipation and right to enfranchisement. She was instrumental in merging the American Woman Suffrage Association (AWSA), formed by Stone, with the National Woman Suffrage Association (NWSA), founded by her and Stanton, to form the National American Woman Suffrage Association (NAWSA). She was also the co-editor, with Stanton, Matilda Joslyn Gage (1826–98) and Ida Husted Harper (1851–1931), of the massive four-volume *History of Woman Suffrage* (1881).

VIRGINIA WOOLF

It may seem anachronistic to refer to Virginia Woolf (1882–1941) as an 'early feminist' along with Wollstonecraft, since her major works (fictional and non-fictional) were written and published in the 1920s and 30s. But the fact remains that the concerns and anxieties that plagued thinkers and activists in the 1840s and the 50s were not comprehensively addressed even in the following decades, so that Woolf experienced and articulated the realities of sexism in matters of employment in 'higher professions', opportunities in higher education, rights to enfranchisement, and even freedom of creative expression.

The political, social and cultural circumstances in England experienced a cataclysmic upheaval with the First World War; its aftershocks were felt in all areas of human experience, including the 'woman question'. Woolf's oeuvre is situated in, and reflective of, this transitional history. It is noteworthy that there are very few feminist writers of import between Wollstonecraft and Woolf, no one alongside Woolf, and no one after Woolf until Simone de Beauvoir (Belsey and Moore). The major categories of feminism, especially those that second-wave feminism engendered – Liberal, Radical, Marxist and Socialist – are not entirely applicable to Woolf's feminism. As Naomi Black, in *Virginia Woolf as Feminist*, points out, 'Her feminism was original, yet firmly rooted in the woman's movement of her time' (7). Woolf remains a pioneer, along with nineteenth-century feminist thinkers, in expressing in her work the politics and history of her age. This justifies the jettisoning of the chronologies and categories in placing Woolf in the history of feminist thought.

Woolf is a pioneering figure in feminist literary theory. *A Room of One's Own* (1929) and *Three Guineas* (1938) comprise important ideas that have influenced feminist writers and thinkers, especially since the 1960s. She finds pervasive inequality among men and women in every level of social, political, economic and literary life. It is topical not just to the time she belonged to, but across time and space. She finds patriarchy in the domestic sphere, in the masculine oppression of wives and daughters; in public spheres of business, law, education and religion; and in the ideological discourses behind imperialism, colonialism and fascism. The natural outcome of patriarchal oppression is the inferiorisation of women. This imbalance of power and 'rule of patriarchy' is, according to Woolf, also perceptible in literature.

A Room of One's Own is a landmark text in feminist literary history. It is a foundational text on gender, sexuality and feminist criticism. It was based on Woolf's lectures delivered to the women students at Cambridge. Woolf chooses a fictional narrative strategy and employs an all encompassing 'I' as the speaking voice which can be 'Mary Beton, Mary Seton, Mary Carmichael'. The main tenet of the treatise is that 'a woman must have money and a room of her own if she is to write fiction' (565). She proposes that women be treated as a separate class altogether, though she is aware of the difference of her location as a middle-class woman from her working-class sisters. Incidentally, *A Room of One's Own* was published a year after full enfranchisement was granted to women. Woolf finds displacement of feminine representation and subjectivity by male authors in patriarchal texts. In order to account for the absence of the female figure in the English Renaissance, Woolf invents the story of 'Judith Shakespeare', the imaginary sister of William Shakespeare. She was as gifted as her brother, but her creative abilities could not be realised due to her gender. The fact that she had a female face and body countermanded any possibility of Judith living the life of a writer. Woolf also underlines the difficulty that women encounter as readers with male writers asserting their masculine self in the narratorial 'I'. Woolf critiques the exclusion of women from literary language and emphasises the incongruity between the material 'reality' of women and its symbolic presentation in literature. She points out, 'Some of the most inspired words, some of the most profound thoughts in literature fall from her lips; in real life she could scarcely spell and was the property of her husband' (590). Woolf points out the importance of social history that must precede feminist literary history. Woolf accentuates the influence of socialisation processes resulting in the internalisation of a gendered ideology that impedes the fulfillment of women's creative abilities. The ideals of the 'angel of the house' were predominantly understood as proper feminine behaviour; women of the middle and upper classes tended to adhere to their inscribed roles which thwarted their creative aspirations. Condescension and discrimination informed the reception of literature produced by women. Following Coleridge, Woolf puts forward a model of androgyny for the artist in whom 'one must be womanly-man or man-womanly' (624). At the same time, however, she insists on a gendered language for writing about women. She contends that the creative power of women, 'differs greatly from the creative power of men . . . it would be a thousand pities if women wrote like men, or lived like men, or looked like men. . . . Ought not education to bring out and fortify the differences rather than the similarities?' (617) These contradictory ideas unsettle the assumptions about Woolf's treatise presenting a theory of androgyny as a model. In another section of the essay, Woolf describes a creative and vital friendship between two women in a contemporary imaginary novel: 'Chloe liked Olivia. They shared a laboratory together' (614). Here, Woolf presents an interesting insight into the possibilities of a counter-discourse inherent in the material reality of marginality. She argues that since women occupy a marginal position in society, they are unrestrained by detrimental emotions like ambition or patriotism. This leaves women free to create an alternative space of creativity. In *Three Guineas*, Woolf enjoins women, especially daughters of educated women, to form a 'society for outsider', to provide a counter-discourse to patriarchy. She questions the idea of canon-formation which essentially excludes women writers from its purview. In order to understand and analyse the significance of women's literature across time, Woolf exhorts us to unearth forgotten or unknown texts written by women.

★★★★

This chapter has explored the activities and contributions of feminist thinkers of the Anglo-American tradition. This, however, does not imply that feminist questions were not debated in other parts of the world. The condition of women, and the debates and movements related to the alleviation of their condition, in the eastern context, form a special area of inquiry. A separate chapter, titled 'Postcolonial Feminism', is devoted to the analysis of feminism outside the purview of white, Anglo-American perspectives.

SHORT TAKES

OLYMPIA DE GOUGES (1748–93)

Olympia de Gouges, a pioneering feminist, was a playwright, political and social activist, radical thinker and staunch supporter of the ideals of the French Revolution. In 1789, she appeared before the French National Assembly and advocated legal equality, right to education and employment for women. Encouraged by the members of the Society of Republican and Revolutionary Women, she issued a *Declaration of the Rights of Woman and the Female Citizen* in 1791. Here, she brilliantly and forcefully argues that women are free and equal to men. She proposed a 'social contract' that would safeguard women against oppression in marriage. In 1793, de Gouges was executed on charges of sedition.

Germaine de Staël (1766–1817)

An unconventional figure in her life and work, de Staël expressed her opposition against existing patriarchal structures in her novels, *Corinne* and *Delphine*. Her novels champion individual freedom for women and advocate the restructuring of social institutions like marriage. She was a vehement critic of Napoleon for which she was exiled in 1803. Her reputation as a political and literary theorist is derived from *Letters on the Works and Characters of J. J. Rousseau* (1788), *A Treatise on the Influence of the Passions upon the Happiness of Individuals and Nation* (1793) and *A Treatise on Ancient and Modern Literature*.

Aphra Behn (c.1640–89)

Aphra Behn accomplished an extraordinary feat when she became the first woman professional writer in English literature with the performance of her play, *The Forc'd Marriage* (1670). Behn had an unusual and adventurous life – she worked as a spy under the Crown in Antwerp, went to the debtor's prison, and became a prolific writer, earning her livelihood from writing when it was unheard of for a woman. She wrote sixteen plays in all, which were often attacked for being bawdy by her male peers. She challenged the conventional notions of femininity in her plays and in her life. Her reputation as a writer, however, rests on her novel *Oroonoko* (1688), which critiqued the idea of the 'noble savage' and yielded to later postcolonial readings.

Margaret Fuller (1810–50)

Margaret Fuller was the pioneer of the circle of New England women, who were prominent writers, Abolitionists and activists. She was a member of the Transcendentalist group and edited their journal, *The Dial,* from 1840 to 1842. She was also a literary critic and wrote for the *New York Tribune* in 1844. Her first major essay, 'The Great Lawsuit: Man versus Men, Woman versus Women' (1843), was later expanded and revised into a book, *Woman in the Nineteenth Century* (1845). This was a manifesto revealing Fuller's formidable knowledge in literature and philosophy and urging political equality, education and freedom of choice for women. In 1847, she travelled to Italy and became involved with the cause of Italian Revolution under Mazzini. She became romantically attached to an aristocrat, Angelo Ossoli, who was younger to her by several years. It is not clear whether they married or not, but she gave birth to a child out of this association and lived openly with him uncaring of any censure. The family died under tragic circumstances in a shipwreck while they were returning to New York.

HARRIET MARTINEAU (1802–76)

Harriet Martineau is claimed to be the first sociologist. She worked with sociological concepts even before Auguste Comte coined the term 'sociology' to define the systematic study of society, with her outstanding work *Society in America* (1837). The book specially underlines the inferior status of women in America and England by drawing an analogy between their condition and the position of slaves in these societies. She also underscores the oppressive nature of marriage in contemporary society that takes a toll on the health and vigour of women. Apart from being a social commentator, Martineau was a novelist (*The Hour and the Man*) and a writer of children's stories (*The Playfellows*). She wrote a history of England, outlining the events between 1816 and 1846, in *The History of Peace* (1849). Her radical attitude is manifest in *Letters on the Laws of Man's Nature and Development* (1851) that challenged religious dogma. Along with other thinkers of the time – Elizabeth Garret Anderson, Francis Mary Buss – Martineau submitted a petition to the Parliament demanding the right to vote for women. She also advocated the inclusion of women in the medical profession.

THE PANKHURSTS

The Pankhurst family is of special interest in understanding not only the feminist movement but other social and political movements of late-nineteenth and early-twentieth-century England. Emmeline Pankhurst (1858–1928) was a militant suffragist who founded the Women's Social and Political

Union (WSPU). Dr Richard Pankhurst (c.1835–98), husband of Emmeline Pankhurst, drafted the first Suffrage Bill in 1869 and is considered an early feminist. He was also instrumental in formulating the Married Women's Property Act of 1884, which aimed at ending the legal and financial discrimination against married women. Their children, Christabel, Adela and Sylvia, were noted activists and contributed significantly to the suffrage movement in England.

REFERENCES

Annas, Julia. 'Mill and the Subjection of Women.' *Mill's* The Subjection of Women: *Critical Essays*. Ed. Maria H. Morales. Maryland: Rowman and Littlefield Publishers, 2005. Print.

Belsey, Catherine, and Jane Moore. *The Feminist Reader: Essays in Gender and Politics of Literary Criticism*. London: Macmillan, 1997. Print.

Black, Naomi. *Virginia Woolf as Feminist*. New York: Cornell UP, 2004. Print.

Buhle, Mari Jo, and Paul Buhle, ed. *The Concise History of Woman Suffrage*. Illinois: U of Illinois P, 2005. Print.

'Declaration of Sentiments.' The Elizabethan Cady Stanton and Susan B. Anthony Papers Project. Web. 28 October 2014. <http://ecssba.rutgers.edu/docs/seneca.html>.

Mill, John Stuart. 'The Subjection of Women.' *Princeton Readings in Political Thought*. Ed. Mitchell Cohen and Nicole Fermon. New Jersey: Princeton UP, 1996. Print.

Rossi, Alice. *The Feminist Papers: From Adams to Beauvoir*. New York: Columbia UP, 1973. Print.

Wollstonecraft, Mary. *A Vindication of the Rights of Women and a Vindication of the Rights of Men*. New York: Cosimo, 2008.

Woolf, Virginia. *A Room of One's Own: Selected Works of Virginia Woolf*. Hertfordshire: Wordsworth Editions, 2005. Print.

Chapter Two
Simone de Beauvoir and Radical Feminism

Simone de Beauvoir's (1908–86) *The Second Sex*, published in 1949, is an influential treatise that provided intellectual impetus to 'second-wave' feminism. Published five years after women were granted suffrage rights in France, it heralded a new attitude towards rethinking women's position in society. The background against which Beauvoir wrote the book was of inequality and oppression. Women were compelled to yield to the gender stereotypes of being nurturers and homemakers; they were denied financial, political and sexual autonomy and were discriminated against in the labour market. *The Second Sex* focuses on a number of debates and disputes based on existential philosophy and Marxist analysis of history. The two important contentions that emerge from this treatise are:

1. Women have always been relegated to the position of the 'other'; and,
2. Femininity is a construct.

Femininity is traditionally conceived as the 'other' in patriarchal societies, as men have dominated the public sphere. Beauvoir emphasises that, in order to perpetuate patriarchal ideology, men have always assumed the position of 'universal subject', denying women autonomy and agency. She underlines the reality that women are complicit in the continuation of patriarchy:

> When man makes of woman the *Other*, he may, then, expect her to manifest deep-seated tendencies toward complicity. Thus, woman may fail to lay claim to the status of subject because she lacks definite resources, because she feels the necessary bond that ties her to man regardless of reciprocity, and because she is very often well pleased with her role as the *Other*. (xxvii)

The axiom, 'one is not born, but rather, becomes, a woman', that opens the second volume of *The Second Sex*, is based on the concept that existence precedes essence. This is the central tenet of existential philosophy that distinguishes 'being-for-itself' from 'being-in-itself'. Jean Paul Sartre (1905–80), in the essay 'Existentialism and Human Emotions', proposes that there is no predetermined nature or 'essence' that controls, dictates and determines human actions. Rather, it is 'being-for-itself', the freedom of choice and responsibility, that determines and defines one's essence or subjectivity. Following this hypothesis that there is no predetermined, established nature, Beauvoir insists that women internalise certain assumptions about femininity from an early age. This inequality is derived from the biological differences between men and women. Beauvoir has often been accused of glossing over the aspect of sexual difference but she, on the other hand, challenges the patriarchal tendency to assign value to the sexual difference of women in glorifying women's reproductive abilities over their intellectual autonomy. She applies the Hegelian master-slave dialectic to explain the domination-subordination axes that control the lives of men and women. Women are denied selfhood, subjectivity and agency, since they are constructed as an extension of the male 'self'. Men, being physically stronger, have been traditionally engaged in strenuous activities such as hunting, gathering and defending the tribe, while women were involved in the domestic space as nurturers of men and children. This left men free to participate in, and control, the public space. The political, social and economic organisation of society has always favoured the interests of men and sustained the unequal balance of power. Cultural productions are predominantly male activities and traditionally marginalise women. To create, to invent, to innovate have always been recognised as male spheres of experience and engagement. Women were denied access to intellectual autonomy; as a consequence, they have remained passive and subservient. Women were traditionally constrained and inscribed into the roles of mother and wife, which prevented them from engaging in any project or enterprise of transcendence, separate from their biological/sexual identity. Beauvoir argues for economic independence for women that would bring about their emancipation from the bonds of norms and fixed socio-cultural roles.

The sense of 'othering' experienced by women is more complex than the master-slave dialectic. According to Beauvoir, there is a Heideggarian *Mitsein*, or 'being-with-other', in the relationship between men and women. Beauvoir borrows this neologism from Martin Heidegger's (1889–1926) magnum opus, *Being and Time* (1927). It means that an ontological feature of a human being is his/her experience of being part of a fellowship about which one is expected to care. Beauvoir, in *The Second Sex*, claims that women aspire to participate in the human *Mitsein*, thus suggesting that women are part of a pre-existing fellowship that is masculine in nature. Unlike Jews or blacks, women have never identified themselves as a minority group; they could never transcend the immediate context and have always lived 'dispersed' among men. 'The division of the sexes is a biological fact, not an event in human history' (19). Again, women are locked in a conflicting power-play with men along the lines of the 'self-other' dichotomy, but this binary is not always comparable with the 'self-other' duality between man as a subject and other men as a marginalised group. Women, in this sense, are the absolute 'other' because of the unique nature of the social, economic, emotional and domestic links among them: 'The couple is a fundamental unit with its two halves riveted together, and the cleavage of society along the lines of sex is impossible. Here is to be found the basic trait of woman: She is the Other in a totality of which the two components are necessary to one another' (25).

Beauvoir challenges Sigmund Freud's universalised view of female sexuality and 'penis envy'. It is not the lack of penis that causes her alienation, she argues, but rather the realisation of the power and privileges accrued naturally by possession of the penis that causes this split. It is, therefore, not a biological distinction but rather the social construct that causes female anxiety. Some may find biological pessimism in Beauvoir's portrayal of women's experience of embodiment. She insists that women are alienated from transcendence by yielding to their physicality. They become pawns of patriarchy by becoming docile objects of male consumption. Though woman has both productive and reproductive abilities, 'she is for man a sexual partner, a reproducer, an erotic subject – an Other through whom he seeks himself' (90). Women are reduced to a marginal position in the workplace and relegated to their reproductive roles – she is an 'other' in the material and abstract spheres of experience. They are absent or silenced in historical narratives; patriarchal ideology governs the representation of the myth of femininity in cultural forms. Beauvoir examines the presentation of the myth of femininity in the texts of five authors – Paul Claudel, Andre Breton, Stendhal, D. H. Lawrence and Henry de Montherlant. Among these writers Beauvoir finds only Stendhal depicting women as something closer to transcendence, but, predominantly, women are depicted by these authors as the other 'capable of revealing him to himself' (281).

In her treatment of childhood, Beauvoir shows how children are encouraged to adhere to the normative sexual tendencies that contribute to the perpetuation of patriarchy. Gendered identity is instilled early on – boys are encouraged to be boisterous and physically active, while girl children are encouraged to be timid and diffident. Beauvoir exposes the fact that female sexuality is passivised by male desire. Women are passive participants while men occupy active subjectivity in sexual relationships.

Beauvoir's approach towards marriage and motherhood is scathing. Marriage, according to Beauvoir, serves male interests and, therefore, is promoted as a desirable norm. Since contraception and abortion were still inaccessible to women in France, her argument that women could not exercise control over motherhood seems valid. Maternal instinct is a construct, and maternal guilt is imposed by patriarchy over women who are defiant of the stereotypes of motherhood. In an interview with Margaret Simons, Beauvoir clarifies that she has not held motherhood as negative, rather it can be an 'interesting and privileged' (Simons 32) relationship. However, in many cases, it can become an agency of narcissism and tyranny. This is because women, who have been denied autonomy and subjecthood, cannot be entrusted with motherhood without running the risk of perpetuating the unequal power structure inherent in patriarchy. In the chapters, 'The Narcissist', 'The Woman in Love' and 'The Mystic', she analyses the 'inauthentic' roles that women accept. Her treatment of women who seek freedom from deterministic social roles is nuanced and sympathetic: 'The independent woman of today is torn between her professional interests and the problems of her sexual life. It is difficult for her to strike a balance between the two; if she does, it is at the price of concessions and sacrifices which require her to be in a constant state of tension' (705). Women must be economically independent and politically aware to be free to lead an 'authentic life'. Patriarchy imposes the constructs of 'femininity', such as 'maternal instinct', to suppress and marginalise women, to relegate them to the position of the absolute other, denying subjectivity, and rendering them as objects of consumption by the male 'gaze'. Toril Moi, in her review of a translation of *The Second Sex* by Constance Borde and Sheila Malovany-Chevallier (2009), provides an insightful exposition of Beauvoir's text. She states,

> Beauvoir formulates three principles and applies them to women's situation in the world. First is her foundational insight that man 'is the Subject, he is the Absolute: she is the Other'. . . . The next principle is that freedom, not happiness, must be used as the measuring stick to assess the situation of women. . . . Finally, there is the insight that women are not born but made, that every society has constructed a vast material, cultural and ideological apparatus dedicated to the fabrication of femininity. (3–4)

RADICAL FEMINISM

Radical feminism is a part of second-wave feminism that viewed women's oppression as a result of patriarchal assumptions of male supremacy. Oppression is operative on several levels – controlling female sexuality, imposing mandatory motherhood, insisting on normative heterosexuality, etc. Radical feminism identified patriarchy as universal and ahistorical; consequently, women's oppression was viewed as a universal phenomenon subsuming racial and class oppressions. They differed from Liberal and Marxist feminists in their insistence on the necessity of re-configuring society along gender lines. Radical feminists detected the ways by which patriarchy oppressed women in deeply stratified social structures and institutions. They identified childbearing, love, marriage, sexual intercourse and housework as the 'naturalising' systems that perpetuated the oppression of women. Kathie Sarachild explains the meaning of the qualifier 'radical' in Radical feminism: 'The dictionary says radical means root, coming from the Latin word for root. And that is what we meant by calling ourselves radical. We were interested in getting to the roots of the problem in society' (145). Women's personal experiences formed the introductory category for activism and analysis in Radical feminism. This is manifest in the contemporary slogan, 'The personal is political.'

'Consciousness-raising' was an important strategy for the theorists and activists of Radical feminism, especially in small women-only group discussions. Though this process of sharing and analysing one's own experience in a group has been disparaged and belittled as a form of therapy, it was surely a significant way of understanding women's situatedness. It offered rare insights into the materiality of women's experiences and served as a crucial organising tool.

Second-wave feminism is not just the continuation of the first-wave but an expansionist movement as well, including and addressing concerns of women of different classes, races and sexual orientations. 'Feminism', Enke states, 'took shape as a popular movement around the limitations and possibilities of local geographies' as women in the 1960s and 70s 'faced exclusions and hierarchies' entrenched in public spaces (9). Radical feminism emerged from a deep dissatisfaction with the Liberal feminist's inadequacies in explaining the importance of the sex-gender dichotomy in women's oppression. Theorists such as Jo Freeman (b.1945) provided a radical perspective to the masculinity-femininity debate by referring to the 'Bitch' syndrome, which was an androgynous symbol, combining 'masculine' as well as 'feminine' attributes. This extremist view was eschewed by later Cultural feminists in favour of acquiring values and virtues that were culturally ascribed to women. This was assumed to be empowering and liberating for women.

Radical feminists argued that sexism is so deeply embedded in society that political, social and personal equality and justice can be achieved only if radical measures are adopted. Radical feminists maintain that the entire gender system must be transformed in order to eradicate gender oppression. They refuse to relegate issues related to sexuality and reproduction to the realm of the personal or private; these issues are in reality political, since patriarchy structures the oppressive practices around them. Though personal experiences were crucial in giving shape to Radical feminism, it was also greatly influenced by the intellectual elements of the Left ideology, psychotherapy, and Civil Rights and other contemporary social movements. Radical feminists included not only the reformists who joined various organisations and groups to improve women's conditions, but also the revolutionaries who participated in radical movements such as the Civil Rights and the anti-Vietnam War movements. The political movement that shaped second-wave feminism was the Women's Rights Movement (WRM) comprising campaigners fighting to end discrimination against women at the workplace. The New Left, the Civil Rights activists and the anti-Vietnam campaign constituted the Women's Liberation Movement (WLM).

Radical feminism was influenced by several radical political movements, especially by Marxism. Nonetheless, it tried to formulate a separate theoretical discourse within a feminist framework. The accusation that Radical feminism operated within the narrow domain of predominantly white middle-class women is addressed by Stephanie Gilmore, in her anthology *Feminist Coalitions: Historical Perspectives on Second Wave Feminism in the United States*. She insists that feminist movements in the 1960s and 70s involved women of diverse racial and social backgrounds and was not limited only to a small group of white middle-class women. Radical feminism challenged patriarchal, heterosexist norms and practices. It spearheaded the creation of new institutions such as battered women's shelters and rape crisis centres, and facilitated the emergence of new civic spaces such as coffeehouses and bookstores where women could assemble, discuss, organise and celebrate.

Betty Friedan's *The Feminine Mystique* (1963), an important text of second-wave feminism, has been critiqued for its narrow scope of analysis, but it explodes the myth of the 'happy affluent housewife' of the American suburbs. She diagnosed the discontent among the housewives who lead restricted lives. Friedan critiques the idealisation of the traditional roles assigned to women. Her book was based on her personal experiences and the experiences narrated by real women through questionnaires provided by Friedan. The central argument of the book is that since the 1940s, the 'ideal' role for the American woman has emphasised the 'feminine mystique'. 'The feminine mystique', according to Friedan, insists that 'the highest value and the only commitment for women is the fulfillment of their own femininity. . . . Beneath the sophisticated trapping, it simply makes certain concrete, finite domestic aspects of feminine existence . . . into a religion, a pattern by which all women must now live or deny their femininity' (213). Friedan exhorts these women to initiate a process of self-enquiry to seek what they truly want for themselves, apart from stability in marriage, children, sexual gratification and the security of conventional roles. *The Feminine Mystique* is an important text, which marks the shift from the earlier economic analysis based on Marxism to humanistic psychological concerns. It also traces the continuity of the movements of the 1940s and 50s culminating in the second wave of the women's movement.

Juliet Mitchell's *Women's Estate* (1971) is another significant contribution and response to feminist movement and theory. It provides valuable insights into several issues contingent on the 1960s' feminist movement. The book is divided into two parts; the first part reviews the development and background of the women's liberation movement, and its history, preoccupations and contradictions. The first chapter, 'The Background of the 60s', firmly locates the women's movement in its immediate history. The second chapter provides a survey of the development of the movement in North America and Europe. The third chapter deals with the politics of women's liberation with reference to Socialist and Radical feminisms. The first part of the book provides the necessary background for the questions raised in the second section, where Mitchell offers her analysis of the realities of women's oppression. She perceives this oppression as distinctively operative in four spheres – production, reproduction, sexuality and the socialisation of children. Under 'production', Mitchell discusses women's participation in labour outside the 'domestic' or 'family' sphere. Under 'reproduction', she includes the ideas of family, kinship and childbearing, while 'sexuality' surveys other kinds of oppression through indoctrination. 'Socialisation of children' emphasises the covert forms of oppression in the 'cultural vocation' of women vis-à-vis child-rearing. She finds the women's movement potentially revolutionary since it is a struggle of the oppressed.

Shulamith Firestone, another influential second-wave feminist, in *The Dialectic of Sex,* applies the Marxist analysis of class struggle and the base-superstructure dialectic to provide a feminist paradigm to the development of history. She argues that sexuality forms the structural basis of society on which the cultural superstructure is erected. The tension between the base (those who are capable of biological reproduction but have no control over the means of production) and the superstructure (those who are not capable of biological reproduction but control the means of reproduction) has determined and caused the subordination of women. Firestone promulgates a revolutionary thesis for eradicating sexual inequality. She suggests a complete transformation of the structures and institutions of society in order to annihilate the disparities inherent in the different sexual roles of men and women. The most radical proposition put forward by Firestone is to eliminate the biological family structure, to bring about an end to gender, class and race oppression. Firestone points out the connection between the suffrage movement of first-wave feminism and the women's liberation movement of the 1960s. She emphasises that the feminism of the 60s is the second-wave of the most important revolution in history, which aimed at overthrowing the oldest, most rigid class/caste system in existence.

Catherine MacKinnon and Andrea Dworkin studied pornography to identify the pattern of sexual dominance-subordination causative of gender oppression. Pornography, according to MacKinnon, is a signifier of male 'sexual fascism'. She points out,

> From the testimony of pornography, what men want is: women bound, women battered, women tormented, women humiliated, women degraded and defiled, women killed. Or to be fair to the soft core, women sexually accessible, have-able, there for them, wanting to be taken and used, with perhaps, just a little light bondage. Each violation of women – rape, battering, prostitution, child sexual abuse, sexual harassment – is made sexy, fun and liberating of women's true nature in pornography. (166)

Kate Millet finds institutionalised patriarchy in all aspects of society. Sexual inequality is deeply ingrained in religious, social, political and economic structures breeding 'interior colonisation' and pervasive power disparity. In *Sexual Politics* (1970), Millet depicts the power relationship between the sexes constituted around the domination-subordination pattern. She exposes the patriarchal plot that assigns dominant roles to men based on biological differences. Millet underscores the importance of the women's movement of the nineteenth century in challenging patriarchal ideology and ensuring a degree of legal, political and economic rights for women. This, according to Millet, contributed to the progress of twentieth-century feminist movements. She argues that women have been simultaneously idealised and disparaged, substantiating her thesis by referring to the overt misogynistic attitudes of male writers across time and cultures: Freud, D. H. Lawrence, Henry Miller, Norman Mailer and Jean Genet. By insisting on the necessity of accepting that 'personal is political', Millet reconciles the apparently irreconcilable. She scathingly critiques phallic writing focused on gender stereotypes and the sexist language used by male writers. This 'cultural programming', she argues, renders women passive and infantile by concerted patriarchal force. Apart from these 'literary men', Millet also identifies psychologist Sigmund Freud and sociologist Talcott Parson as responsible for the perpetuation of the myth of feminine inferiority. Millet, however, offers an affirmative possibility of a future without the malaise of the sex-gender dichotomy. Her vision of an androgynous existence is not simply an amalgam of traditional attributes categorised as 'masculine' and 'feminine'. Thus, androgyny is not just a combination of 'docility' (an attribute associated with femininity) and arrogance (traditionally ascribed to men), but an amalgam of ideals and virtues that go beyond gender.

In *The Female Eunuch* (1970), Germaine Greer suggests a novel way of dismantling patriarchy. Women should withdraw their labour (women, in this paradigm, are viewed as the proletariat) to render patriarchy dysfunctional. This radicalisation of attitude underlines the importance of unacknowledged domestic labour put in by women that has been historically viewed as inferior, insignificant and free. Greer emphatically points out the sense of inferiority that women passively accept and internalise. She also challenges the myths of love and marriage and exposes the oppressive ideology inherent in the tropes of 'cooking, beauty, clothes and housekeeping' (347).

Mary Daly, in *Gyn/Ecology* (1978), underlines patriarchal oppression via the appropriation of language. Daly challenges sexism by subverting language and creating a separate women's language. Her first book, *The Church and the Second Sex* (1968), caused a great deal of controversy and divided opinions. In *Gyn/Ecology,* she presents patriarchy as a universal force of oppression upon which all other oppressive structures such as colonialism and racism are based:

> Those who claim to see racism and/or imperialism in my indictment of these atrocities [including *sati* and female genital cutting] can do so only blinding themselves to the fact that the oppression of women knows no ethnic, national, or religious bounds. They are variations on the theme of oppression, but the phenomenon is planetary. (111)

Gloria Steinem (b.1934), another significant figure of second-wave feminism, co-founded *Ms.*, a magazine that addresses women's concerns. She helped to establish organisations such as the National Women's Political Caucus and Choice USA, a reproductive rights non-profit organisation. Often attacked by hardliners among the

Radical feminists for being 'middle-class' oriented, Steinem remains a staunch advocate of the Equal Rights Amendment (ERA) to the US Constitution that promises equality to women, abortion rights, equal pay, anti-trafficking movements and movements against domestic violence.

Radical feminism provided the impetus to Cultural feminism, which followed it and tried to bridge certain gaps in the former. Ellen Willis has pointed out some of the reasons that contributed to the dismantling of Radical feminism:

> Many women reacted to radical feminism with an intense desire to change their lives, or the social arrangements that immediately affected them, but had no intention of supporting changes that would threaten their (or their husbands') economic and social class status. Many of the same women were reluctant to explicitly attack male power – not only because of the personal consequences of militancy, but because the whole subject of power is uncomfortable for people who are basically committed to the existing socioeconomic order. (107)

Radical feminism added a sense of urgency to the contemporary feminist movement by putting issues related to sexual politics and equality in the public and private spheres, at the centre of the feminist debate. Radical feminism was also characterised by consciousness-raising against institutional powers, mass movements organised to strengthen women's demands for dignity and personhood, and rebellion against the restrictions imposed by patriarchal structures. Radical feminism contributed to the transformation of women's consciousness in the 1960s and 70s.

REDSTOCKINGS

Redstockings, an influential feminist group established in 1969 by Shulamith Firestone and Ellen Willis, was the first group to publicly espouse Radical feminism. It brought together two traditions, supplanting the 'blue' of the 'bluestockings' (which was a disparaging term used for the first-generation feminists) with 'red' representing overt Left ideology. The group was organised by Firestone and Willis, after breaking away from

SHORT TAKES

the New York Radical Women organisation. Other members included Kathie Sarachild, Corrine Grad Cleman, Carol Hanisch and Irene Peslikis. 'The Redstockings Manifesto', published in 1969, called for unity of women to dismantle the inequalities and injustices of the male-dominated society. Apart from insisting upon the importance of the personal experiences of women, the Redstockings also dismissed the assumption that systems (like the family or Capitalism) are autonomous. They argued that these systems need not be mystified as agencies which operate on both the oppressor and the oppressed by some abstract logic unconnected to either. This actually excused men from their responsibility in women's oppression. Members of the Redstockings were also sceptical of lesbian separatism which they interpreted as a political identity rather than a personal identity. They advocated the 'pro-woman line', 'sisterhood', activism, and the public 'speaking out' against such taboo subjects as abortion. The Redstockings group maintains a historical collection, the Redstockings Women's Liberation Movement Archives for Action.

NEW YORK RADICAL FEMINIST GROUP

The New York Radical Feminist Group was organised by Shulamith Firestone and Anne Koedt with the Stanton-Anthony Brigade, in 1969, after they and other members had left the Redstockings and The Feminist respectively. The formation of the group was facilitated by Vivian Gornick's 1969 essay, 'The Next Great Moment in History is Theirs', published in *Village Voice*. The ideology of this group challenged the preoccupations of other Radical feminists as embodied in the 'pro-woman line' of the Redstockings and the emphasis on women's unconscious playing a greater role in internalising submissive roles, espoused by The Feminists. The New York Radical Feminist Group held that men deliberately dominated women to reinforce their egotistic sense of superiority and women consciously abnegate their egos to embrace diffident sex roles. The group organised ten to twelve women consciousness-raising groups throughout New York City. They took on such issues as sexual assault, molestation, marriage and motherhood. The group held a conference on rape in the spring of 1971, spearheaded by Susan Brownmiller who later published her iconic book on this issue, *Against Our Will: Women and Rape*, in 1975.

REFERENCES

Daly, Mary. *Gyn/Ecology: The Metaethics of Radical Feminism*. Boston: Beacon Press, 1990. Print.
de Beauvoir, Simone. *The Second Sex*. Trans. H. M. Parshley. New York: Vintage, 1989. Print.
Enke, Anne. *Finding the Movement: Sexuality, Contested Space, and Feminist Activism*. Durham: Duke UP, 2007. Print.
Firestone, Shulamith, *The Dialectic of Sex: The Case for a Feminist Revolution*. New York: Bantam Books, 1970. Print.
Friedan, Betty. 'The Feminist Mystique.' *America since 1945*. Ed. Robert D. Marcus and David Burnes. New York: St Martin's Press, 1991. Print.
Greer, Germaine. *The Female Eunuch*. London: Harper Perennial, 2006. Print.
MacKinnon, Catherine. 'Sexuality.' *The Second Wave: A Reader in Feminist Theory*. Ed. I. Nicholson. New York: Routledge, 1997. Print.
Moi, Toril. 'The Adulteress Wife.' *London Review of Books* 3.11 (February 2010). Web. 29 October 2014. <www.lrb.co.uk/v32/no3/toril-moi/the-adultress-wife>.
Mitchell, Juliet. *Women's Estate*. London: Penguin, 1971. Print.
Sarachild, Kathie. 'Conscious Raising: A Radical Weapon.' *Feminist Revolution*. New York: Random House, 1975. Print.
Simons, M. A. 'Two Interviews with Simone de Beauvoir' *Revaluing French Feminism*. Ed. N. Fraser and S. I. Bartky. Bloomington: Indiana UP, 1992. Print.
Willis, Ellen. 'Radical Feminism and Feminist Radicalism.' *Social Text* 9/10, *The 60s Without Apology* (Spring–Summer 1984), Duke UP. Web. 29 October 2014. <http://www.jstor.org/stable/466537>.

Chapter Three
Cultural Feminism and Gynocriticism

Cultural feminism bridged the gaps in Radical feminism, especially in providing the psychological reasoning behind the male violence against women. Cultural feminists extended the argument put forward by Radical feminists that rape and other forms of sexual violence were ways of perpetuating male dominance, to the analysis of the representation of sexual violence in media and pornography. Cultural feminists agree with Liberal feminists that material change must be brought about in women's condition but not by compromising their instinctive, intuitive nature. They challenge the existing norms of love, marriage and sexuality, and call for social transformations to realise the demands for women's rights to equality. Cultural feminists underscore the exclusive nature of 'feminine' values – of sympathy, gentleness and non-violence – which need not be repressed. This leads to a more holistic vision of life through reconciliation and harmony.

Cultural feminists seek a complete transformation of the social order by decentring androcentrism in private and public spheres. Charlotte Perkins Gilman (1860–1935), the American writer, feminist and sociologist influenced by Social Darwinism, resists the assumption that women need marriage for survival; dependence on men in marriage and mothering is perceived as unnatural since mothering and domestic work do not require dependence on men. Nancy Chodorow, in *The Reproduction of Mothering*, contends that gender identity is developed within the psychological context of the mother-child relationship. Gendered personality traits of independence and aggression of men, and dependence and emotional intensity in women, determine their role and function in the material reality of society. Men are enabled to negotiate the capitalist world of production, while women are prepared for the domestic sphere and the functions of reproduction. Carol Gilligan bases her thesis of moral reasoning on the models provided by Chodorow. Women's 'mode of thinking . . . is contextual and narrative rather than formal and abstract' (Gilligan 19). Man's morality of rights privileges the individual over the relational, while women's morality is governed by the web of relations surrounding her.

Sara Ruddick's *Maternal Thinking* analyses the implications of the compulsory childbearing role assigned to women. Ruddick argues that a special kind of consciousness emerges from the specific female traditions and practices related to childbearing. She insists that 'maternal thinking' is different from the scientific thought process that governs patriarchal discourse. Ruddick uses the term 'holding' to signify the maternal attitude of nurturance and preservation towards children. She states, 'The recognition of the priority of holding over acquiring . . . distinguishes maternal from scientific thought, as well as from the instrumentation of technocratic capitalism' (350). The maternal ethic presupposes a reverential respect and acceptance of the process of life.

GYNOCRITICISM

Gynocriticism was directed towards the formulation of a 'women's poetics', emphasising the significance of women as writers. It entailed a sympathetic reading of female texts and identifying the gaps in canonical texts, which were considered crucial for feminist criticism. 'Feminine', as a literary trope, along with language and its relationship with the male and female psyche, are the major concerns for gynocritics. Gynocriticism engages with the recovery of lost texts by women writers and explores the difference they make in the existing literary tradition. In 1979, Susan Sniadar Lanser and Evelyn Torton Beck insisted that 'an autonomous woman-centred epistemology' (qtd. in Donovan 99) must constitute the basis of gynocriticism. This was in opposition to the 'androcentric epistemology' predominant in literary theory. In 1980, Michele Barrett urged feminist critics to address the female literary tradition and determine its distinctive aesthetic value. In 1982, Elaine Showalter coined the term 'gynocriticism', a tradition of feminist criticism which focuses on 'women as writers. . . . The subjects are the history, styles, themes, genres, and structures of writing by women; the psychodynamics of female creativity; the trajectory of the individual and collective female career; and the evolution or laws of a female literary tradition' (qtd. in Lennox 81).

Gynocriticism is the branch of feminist criticism that focuses on women's art, with the aim of developing a 'women's poetics'. Lawrence Lipking, in 1983, pointed out the dearth of a theory that is grounded on, and seeks to analyse, a female literary tradition. In continuity with Virginia Woolf's speculations about Shakespeare's sister, Lipking ponders on the silence about Aristotle's sister, Arimneste, in the literary tradition. He points out that classical theory has seldom acknowledged the existence of two sexes. This tendency is brought about by the assumption that women might read and interpret literature differently and in their own way. Lipking suggests that a female epistemology and poetics can be identified and developed from their cultural and social expressions, such as poems, novels, plays, essays and pamphlets, and even from women's conversations. What needs to be avoided is the masculine model of understanding and analysis. Lipking offers a theory on the 'poetics of abandonment', derived from the analysis of Madame de Staël's sentimental novels. The plots of these novels revolved around the seduction and abandonment of young innocent women. Lipking identifies in this iterative motif of abandonment, clues for analysing female creativity, imagery and symbolism. Lipking's theory is useful in understanding a particular kind of women's literature. Universalist assumptions and models for women's poetics cannot accommodate the immense diversity of women's experiences across races, cultures and classes. Gynocriticism ensures the articulation of voices hitherto silenced, expressing that which has not been expressed.

The Caribbean-American writer and feminist, Audre Lorde's dictum, 'the master's tools will never dismantle the master's house', is quite relevant to gynocriticism, since it underlines and subverts the androcentric perceptions that dominate interpretations of literature. The second wave of feminism ushered in a reinterpretation and critique of what was held as 'phallic writing' and sought to analyse the ways in which gender stereotypes of 'hysteria' and 'passivity' were ascribed to women. Judith Fetterley, in *The Resisting Reader* (1978), attacks canonical writers such as Henry James, William Faulkner and F. Scott Fitzgerald for perpetuating these stereotypes.

From 1970 onwards, gynocriticism emerged as a definite approach to reading women-related themes and women writers. Ellen Moer's *Literary Women* (1976) was one of the foundational texts on feminist criticism tracing a female literary tradition. Other influential texts were Tillie Olsen's *Silences* (1978) and Adrienne Rich's *The Dream of a Common Language* (1978). In *A Literature of Their Own* (1977), Elaine Showalter examined the exclusion and marginalisation of the women's literary tradition by focusing on lesser-known nineteenth-century writers such as Sarah Grand and George Egerton. She proposed a tripartite progression of a literary counter-tradition, which she identified as 'feminine', 'feminist' and 'female'. In 'Towards a Feminist Poetics' (1979) and 'Feminist Criticism in Wilderness' (1981), Showalter developed her ideas further to produce two distinct categories in feminist criticism: (a) the woman reader as a consumer of literature, and (b) the woman author, the producer of literature. She also proposed a model of gynocriticism based on four models of gender difference – biological, linguistic, psychoanalytic and cultural.

Gynocriticism is often permeated with a sense of binary oppositions, of the masculine tradition as the 'self' and the female tradition as the 'other', without addressing the complexity inherent in the category 'other'. But it initiated a debate and generated a discourse on female aesthetics. Sandra Gilbert and Susan Gubar, in *The Madwoman in the Attic* (1979) and in the three volumes of *No Man's Land* (1989, 1991, 1994), focus on the marginalisation, exclusion and control of women in literary representations. Stevi

Jackson enumerates the concerns of gynocriticism, 'Feminist criticism proved firstly that literature was not simply a collection of great texts but was deeply structured by social/sexual ideologies, and secondly, that certain preoccupations and techniques predominate in women's writings in relation to those social structures' (qtd. in Humm 198). Gilbert and Gubar use the perspectives of psycho-history and pathology to analyse the work of Jane Austen, the Brontë sisters, Emily Dickinson and George Eliot. They turn the androcentric paradigms of criticism inside out by challenging the trope of 'the anxiety of influence', which Harold Bloom insists is an Oedipal struggle that male authors have to negotiate vis-à-vis their paternal ancestors. Gilbert and Gubar create the author's double in 'the mad woman in the attic'. In *No Man's Land*, they move deeper and farther in their feminist critical approach. They find the sexual imagery of rape and impotence iterative throughout modernist writings by men.

Toril Moi, in *Sexual/Textual Politics*, concentrates on two main fields of feminist theory – the Anglo-American group comprising figures such as Kate Millet, Ellen Moers and Showalter and the French theorists such as Hélène Cixous, Luce Irigaray and Julia Kristeva. *Sexual/Textual Politics* draws attention to the interface between feminism and literature. Literary texts, apart from providing aesthetic pleasure, are also storehouses of ideological contestation. A feminist analysis of these conflicts and contradictions provides insights into the realities and representations of gender, difference and power hierarchy in society. Moi traces the shift from Millet's *Sexual Politics* in understanding the essentialist representation of women in literature, to Showalter's attempts towards rediscovering a women-centred approach in women's writing. Her discussions of Irigaray, Cixous and Kristeva are illuminating vis-à-vis their revolutionary contribution to feminist criticism. However, Moi's text is accused of omitting black feminists and lesbian writings. Her aim is to identify the dialectics of power between sexual and textual politics, and move beyond the binaries of black/white, homosexuality/heterosexuality, and masculinity/femininity. Moi emphasises the necessity of identifying and deconstructing 'textual' politics (which is an insidious way of essentialising the category 'woman'), alongside exposing 'sexual' politics. This, Moi says, can be a more radical and revolutionary approach towards textual production from a feminist perspective.

Poststructuralists have disparaged Gynocriticism for its excessive reliance on women's experiences as the central tenet for criticism. They also find a lack of theoretical finesse in gynocriticism with its excessive dependence on nineteenth-century texts. But it is inarguable that gynocriticism appeared at an important stage in feminist criticism and contributed to the revival and recovery of forgotten and overlooked female texts.

> ### SOCIAL DARWINISM
>
> Social Darwinism is contingent on the doctrine of the struggle for existence and the survival of the fittest. Social Darwinists developed their theories from Charles Darwin's theories of evolution, put forward in his *On the Origin of Species* (1859) and *The Descent of Man* (1871). Herbert Spencer (1820–1903) was an early Social Darwinist who coined the phrase, 'the survival of the fittest'. American industrialist Andrew Carnegie (1835–1919) was a noted champion of the philosophy of Social Darwinism. After the 1880s, Reform Darwinism rose to prominence advocating changes in social and governmental policies addressing the principles of evolution. Eugenics based its principles of superiority on an extreme form of Social Darwinism. Hitler is known to have used eugenic arguments to justify the Holocaust. Important women intellectuals, such as Olive Schreiner (1855–1920) and Charlotte Perkins Gilman (1860–1935), used the concepts of Social Darwinism in their books. Gilman's *Women and Economics* (1898) and Schreiner's *Woman and Labour* (1911) emphasised the importance of 'feminine' virtues of love, co-operation and generosity.

REFERENCES

Chodorow, Nancy J. *The Reproduction of Mothering.* Berkeley: U of California P, 1999. Print.

Donovan, Josephine. 'Towards a Women's Poetics.' *Tulsa Studies in Women's Literature* 13.1/2, Feminist Issues in Literary Scholarship (Spring–Autumn 1984). U of Tulsa. Web. 11 December 2013. <http://www.jstor.org/stable/463827>.

Gilbert, Sandra M., and Susan Gubar. *The Madwoman in the Attic: The Woman Writer and the Nineteenth Century Literary Imagination.* New Haven: Yale UP, 1979. Print.

---. *No Man's Land: The Place of the Woman Writer in the Twentieth Century. Vol 1. The War of the Words.* New Haven: Yale UP, 1989. Print.

---. *No Man's Land: The Place of the Woman Writer in the Twentieth Century. Vol 2. Sexchanges.* New Haven: Yale UP, 1991. Print.

---. *No Man's Land: The Place of the Woman Writer in the Twentieth Century. Vol 3. Letters from the Front.* New Haven: Yale UP, 1994. Print.

Gilligan, Carol. *In a Different Voice.* Cambridge: Harvard UP, 2009. Print.

Humm, Maggie. 'Feminist Literary Tradition.' *Contemporary Feminist Theories.* Ed. Stevi Jackson. Edinburgh: Edinburgh Press, 1996. Print.

Lennox, Sara. *Cemetery of the Murdered Daughters: Feminism, History and Ingeborg Bachmann.* Massachusetts: U of Massachusetts P, 2006. Print.

Lipking, Lawrence. 'Aristotle's Sister: A Poetics of Abandonment.' *Critical Inquiry* 10 (September 1983): 63. Print.

Moi, Toril. *Sexual/Textual Politics: Feminist Literary Theory.* New York: Methuen, 1985. Print.

Ruddick, Sara. 'Maternal Thinking.' *Feminist Studies* 6 (Summer 1980): 346. Print.

Chapter Four
Marxist and Socialist Feminism

It is difficult to distinguish between Marxist feminism and Socialist feminism, but the fundamental agenda that differentiates them is that while Marxist feminism perceives class as the central factor for the social and economic oppression of women, Socialist feminism finds both gender and class as contributing factors. Sexuality and reproduction are also considered crucial agents of discrimination. Socialist feminism widened the scope of analysis and response to the reality of women's oppression by focusing on female sexuality and mothering as important and determining factors of power hierarchy in the gendered relations of society.

In Marxist analysis, history progresses through the dialectic of base (economic or material) and superstructure (politico-legal ideology, philosophy, religion and culture). Feminists use a 'dual-system' method by which they view women's oppression issuing from both the economic or material base of society on the one hand, and patriarchy on the other. Heidi Hartmann, in her essay 'The Unhappy Marriage of Marxism and Feminism' (1981), underscores the patriarchal base of society (distinct from the material base) that operates through the control over women's sexual and domestic labour in both public and private spheres. In the public sphere, women are paid less, and in the private sphere, they are consigned to the drudgery of domestic labour which has use-value but no exchange-value. Further, capitalism is congruent with patriarchy wherein men are paid enough, so that women are kept within the family fold and are compelled to engage in housework. In this structure, women are comparable to the proletariat in a capitalist system. Patriarchy produces a similar ideology in capitalism where women are viewed as 'dependents'. The role of 'nurturer' that women accept for themselves demeans their rank in society, since their function does not yield exchange-value. It only has use-value, which is inadequate and inferior within the capitalist paradigm. Thus, sexism is compounded with capitalism to oppress women.

The relationship between Marxism and feminism is emphasised by Catherine MacKinnon, in the essay 'Feminism, Marxism, Method, and the State: An Agenda for Theory':

> Marxism and feminism are theories of power and its distribution: inequality. They provide accounts of how social arrangements of patterned disparity can be internally rational yet unjust. But their specificity is not incidental. In Marxism to be deprived of one's work, in feminism of one's sexuality, defines each one's conception of lack of power per se. They do not mean to exist side by side to insure that two separate spheres of social life are not overlooked, the interest of two groups are not obscured, or the contributions of two sets of variables are not ignored. (516–17)

Feminists, across time, have sought to accommodate and modify Marxist ideas to explain the phenomenon of women's subordination. This resulted in serious contestation about the relationship between patriarchy and capitalism. Feminists were divided over the contentious issue of identifying whether patriarchy or capitalism was responsible for women's oppression. While classical Marxist feminism sought to understand gender inequality according to stringent Marxist notions of class disparity, Radical and Socialist feminists reworked the Marxist theoretical framework to contribute to the conceptual paradigm of feminism. If capitalism is perceived as a power relationship, all relationships are fundamentally exploitative, including those that women share with their employers and families.

Capitalism is exploitative since workers are paid only for their labour and not for the real value of the commodities produced by their energy and intelligence. Marx's ideas of class and class consciousness, when applied to the feminist framework, raise several pertinent questions. The most important among them being whether women, with their heterogeneous and dispersed location, can be considered as a single class. Many Marxist and Socialist feminists believe that women can form a separate class despite their apparent differences. For women, the sense of alienation is more pronounced. As Ann Foreman, in *Femininity as Alienation: Women and the Family in Marxism and Psychoanalysis*, states,

> The man exists in the social world of business and industry as well as in the family and therefore is able to express himself in these different spheres. For the woman, however, her place is within the home. Men's objectification within industry, through the expropriation of the product of their labour, takes the form of alienation. But the effect of alienation on the lives and consciousness of women takes an even more oppressive form. Men seek relief from their alienation through their relations with women; for women there is no relief. For these intimate relations are the very ones that are essential structures of her oppression. (qtd. in Tong 102)

In *The Origin of Family, Private Property, and the State* (1845), Friedrich Engels delineated the decline of the matrilineal and matriarchal society and the rise of patriarchy, with the paradigm shift in economic production and private property possession. He insisted that before family and familial relationship existed, men and women had absolute sexual freedom. This 'promiscuous' interaction decreased with men claiming possession of individual women to ensure property rights and inheritance of biological children. The change in the system of production caused a gradual decline in women's importance in society. With the increase in production outside the house, sexual division of labour intensified, leading to the 'overthrow of the mother right' which Engels argues was 'the world-historic defeat of the female sex' (qtd. in Lerner 21). Women became 'slaves' to male sexual desire and economic dominance. The husband represented the bourgeoisie and the wife represented the proletariat. Monogamy too, according to Engels, was based on economic conditions; ideas of love and commitment were subordinate to the power structure of patriarchy. Engels insisted on economic freedom for women in order to subvert the patriarchal power-play. He also believed that proletarian women suffered less oppression than bourgeois women. Engels was virulent in his condemnation of the bourgeois concept of marriage, or the 'marriage of convenience', which he said 'often enough turns into the crassest prostitution – sometimes on both sides, but much more generally on the part of the wife, who differs from the ordinary courtesan only in that she does not hire out her body, like a wageworker, on piece-work, but sells it into slavery once and for all' (Engels 78). He found greater equality in proletarian marriages, since women of that class were generally employed outside their domestic sphere leading to a degree of gender equality.

Classical Marxist feminists emphasise class analysis to explain gender oppression. Theorists such as Evelyn Reed argue that men's oppression of women, or women's oppression of women, is caused by class disparity. Reed dismisses the possibility of women forming a class, since capitalism, not patriarchy, is the enemy of gender equality. Classical Marxist feminism believed that a communist society heralding the end of capitalism would ensure equality among men and women. But the reality of post-Communist societies differed from this idealised vision. Women were expected to do housework along with participating in the workforce, since the socialisation of domestic work was unmediated. Sexual division of labour, both in the public and private spheres, continued unabated, thereby contradicting the classical Marxist feminist formulations of gender equality. Rosemary Hennessy points out,

> One of Marxist feminism's main contributions to class analysis lies in what have come to be known as the domestic labour debates. This work was an effort to address the ways in which labour done outside the market-place of wage economy under capitalism, and most often relegated to women, can be explained in terms of the socially necessary benefits it provides to capital and its place in the capitalist class system. (64)

Theorists such as Maria Della Costa and Selma James campaigned for 'wage-for-housework' as the only way to annihilate the economic disparity along gender lines in a capitalist society. This argument was, however, found unfeasible on several counts; the 'wage-for-housework' campaign reinforced the sexual division of labour and subverted the socialisation of domestic work.

SOCIALIST OR MATERIALIST FEMINISM

Socialist or Materialist feminists find patriarchy equally implicated as capitalism in perpetuating women's oppression. Material feminism emerged in the 1960s with the convergence of Marxism and feminism. Material feminism extended its scope of investigation from class analysis to include race, ethnicity, nationality, sexuality and religion in understanding gender oppression. Juliet Mitchell's essay, 'Women: The Longest Revolution' (1966), which was later expanded to the book *Women's Estate* (1971), revises the traditional Marxist feminist framework by underscoring the importance of psychoanalysis along with class analysis in explaining women's oppression. Mitchell points out the intersection of patriarchy and capitalism in the exploitation of women:

> Men enter into the class dominated structure of history while women (as women, whatever their work in actual production) remain defined by the kinship pattern of organization. Differences of class, historical epoch, specific social situation alter the expression of femininity; but in relation to the law of the father, women's position across the board is a comparable one. (409)

Early Marxist feminists such as Clara Zetkin (1857–1933), Isaac Babel (1894–1940) and Alexandra Kollontai (1872–1952) championed the emancipation of women by eradicating class distinctions. Subsequently, Marxist feminists identified those social structures through which women were exploited and oppressed. Socialist feminists differed from the classical Marxist point of view in their understanding of the relationship between class struggle and women's struggle. In this context, gender ideology emerged as an important feature of analysis along with the effects of capitalism. Michele Barrett's *Women's Oppression Today: The Marxist/Feminist Encounter* (1988) is an important work of Materialist feminism. In an essay titled 'Ideology and the Cultural Production of Gender', included in the book, Barrett emphasises the centrality of ideology in gender construction; that provides a fresh interface between Marxism and feminism. Gender ideology comprised the belief system that women's oppression is natural. The Althusserian enunciation of ideology provides the necessary impetus to this framework. Barrett argues that the analysis of women's oppression from the perspective of capitalism and/or patriarchy does not always include the role of ideology in constructing identity, subjectivity and a social system. She expresses dissatisfaction with Cultural feminism's assumption of the biological difference between men and women, as well as classical Marxist feminism's oversimplification of ideology as merely a reflection of dominant modes of production. Barrett contends that ideology not only refers to class relations but is constructed by race, ethnicity and different forms of labour.

FEMINIST STANDPOINT THEORY

Feminist Standpoint theorists such as Nancy Hartsock, Sandra Harding and Patricia Hill Collins argue that knowledge is socially situated, and that marginalised groups have a better understanding of reality. This theoretical approach emerged from an interaction between Marxism and feminism in the 1970s. Feminist Standpoint theorists underscored the importance of women's lived experiences as the material basis for understanding power relations and the construction of knowledge. They believed that the sociopolitical position occupied by women (and other marginalised groups) can generate particular knowledges, not only about themselves but also about the oppressors. Alison M. Jaggar points out, 'The pervasiveness and relentlessness of their suffering pushes oppressed groups to find out what is wrong with the prevailing order and develop new and less distorted ways of seeing the world' (56). This is a reflection of the Marxist framework of epistemology which can only be determined from one's social (class) position. According to this thesis, the bourgeoisie standpoint would be different from the proletarian standpoint.

The Standpoint feminists contend that women's unique social position and gendered division of labour provide clues to an analysis of the kinds of oppression that they experience. Sandra Harding argues, 'Starting off research from women's lives will generate less partial and distorted accounts not only of women's lives but also of men's lives and of the whole social order' (56). The Standpoint feminists point out that women are expected to assume the primary responsibilities of nurturance, thereby yielding to an unequal power relation with the dominant group. This social positioning, and not any innate quality, acts as an epistemic agent. As Sara Ruddick points out, the nurturing skill of women that are held 'natural' to their sex is essentially a consequence of the fact that women from a very young age have internalised the role of the care-giver assigned to them by dominant groups.

> ### ALEXANDRA KOLLONTAI (1872–1952)
>
> Alexandra Kollontai was a Russian communist revolutionary and thinker who actively participated in the 1917 Revolution and the events thereafter. Kollontai was an iconoclast in her radical attitude towards sexuality and family. She considered family life to be perpetuating the oppressive property-based structures, causing the subjugation of women. Kollontai is known for her work among Russian working-class women around the 1917 Revolution. Her important works are 'Women Fighters in the Days of the Great October Revolution', 'International Women's Day', 'The Worker's Opposition', 'On the History of the Movement of Women Workers in Russia', 'Communism and the Family' and 'Several Relations and Class Struggle'. In 'The Social Basis of the Woman Question', Kollontai disparages both bourgeois feminism and the separatist women's movement and argues in favour of women's struggle for their own rights within the structures of social democratic parties. After the Second Revolution of 1917, Kollontai played a crucial role in drafting legislations for civil marriage, easy divorce, labour protection and equal pay for women.

> ### IDEOLOGY
>
> Karl Marx defines 'ideology' in his Preface to *A Contribution to the Critique of Political Economy* as 'false consciousness', since it does not deal with the real material conditions of life but engages with the analysis of abstract ideals of truth, beauty and spirit. He states, 'It is not the consciousness of men that determines their

being, but on the contrary, their social being that determines their consciousness.' Ideology is, therefore, related to the realities of class, class consciousness and power. Later Marxist critics have found this analysis of ideology reductive and economically determined. Twentieth-century Marxist philosopher Louis Althusser argues that ideology is autonomous from economics or the classical Marxist 'base'. Recent thinkers such as Ernesto Laclou and Chantal Mouffe have emphasised the importance or relevance of social movements in analysing ideology, citing the inadequacy of the Marxist base/superstructure model in incorporating movements which are not entirely bound by economic relations.

BOURGEOIS AND PROLETARIAT

Karl Marx and Friedrich Engels, in *The Communist Manifesto*, defined society according to class structure, class consciousness and emanation of power. Engels, in a footnote in *The Communist Manifesto*, defined 'bourgeois' as that class which owns the means of production and can buy labour power. Proletariats are wage-labourers or industrial labourers who do not own the means of production but sell their labour in lieu of wages from the bourgeoisie. Marx mentions another transitional class of people, the *petit bourgeois*, who own sufficient modes of production but cannot buy labour power. The class struggle is, however, rife between the proletariat and the bourgeoisie, which Marx envisions would lead to the proletariat seizing the means of production for themselves, thereby creating a new order in society.

REFERENCES

Barrett, Michele. *Women's Oppression Today: The Marxist/Feminist Encounter*. London: Verso, 1980. Print.

Engels, Friedrich. *The Origin of the Family, Private Property and the State*. Abercrombie: Resistance Books, 2004. Print.

Harding, Sandra. 'Rethinking Standpoint Epistemology: What is Strong Objectivity.' *Feminist Epistemologies*. Ed. L. Alcoff and E. Potter. New York: Routledge, 1993. Print.

Hartmann, Heidi. 'The Unhappy Marriage of Marxism and Feminism: Towards a More Progressive Union.' *Women and Revolution: A Discussion of the Unhappy Marriage of Marxism and Feminism.* Ed. Lydia Sargent. Boston: South End, 1981. Print.

Hennessy, Rosemary, 'Class.' *Feminist Theory.* Ed. Mary Eagleton. Malden: Blackwell Publishing Ltd, 2003. Print.

Jaggar, Alison M. 'Feminist Politics and Epistemology: The Standpoint of Women.' *The Feminist Standpoint Theory Reader: Intellectual and Political Controversies.* Ed. Sandra Harding. New York: Routledge, 2004. Print.

Lerner, Gerda. *The Creation of Patriarchy, Vol. 1.* New York: Oxford UP, 1986. Print.

MacKinnon, Catherine A. 'Feminism, Marxism, Method and the State: An Agenda for Theory.' *Signs* 17.3, Feminist Theory (Spring 1982). The U of Chicago P. Web. 30 October 2014. <http://www.jstor.org/stable/3173853>.

Mitchell, Juliet. *Psychoanalysis and Feminism.* New York: Vintage Books, 1975. Print.

Reed, Evelyn. 'Women: Caste, Class or Oppressed Sex?' *International Socialist Review* 31.3 (September 1970): 15–17, 40–41. Print.

Tong, Rosemarie. *Feminist Thought: A More Comprehensive Introduction.* Colorado: Westview Press, 2009. Print.

Chapter Five
Postmodern Feminism

Both feminism and postmodernism are theoretical discourses that are porous, decentred and dynamic. The interface of postmodernism and feminism is, hence, rich and complex. Craig Owens, in his essay 'The Discourse of Others: Feminists and Postmodernism' (1985), points out the absence of a feminist theory per se, even though feminist cultural, political and aesthetic practices are evident. Owens intends to explore the intersection of postmodernism and feminism, introducing the idea of sexual difference into the debate. Modernism, with its emphasis on representational modes, is challenged by the 'decentered, allegorical, schizophrenic' (57) postmodernism:

> Among those prohibited from Western representation, whose representations are denied all legitimacy, are women. Excluded from representation by its very structure, they return within it as a figure for – a representation of – the unrepresentable (Nature, Truth, the Sublime, etc.). This prohibition bears primarily on woman as the subject, and rarely as the object of representation, for there is certainly no shortage of images of women. Yet in being represented by, women have been rendered an absence within the dominant culture. . . . (59)

Postmodern feminism is built upon the ideas of Michel Foucault (1926–84), Jacques Derrida (1930–2004), Jacques Marie Émile Lacan (1901–81) and Simone de Beauvoir. They reject the binarism inherent in patriarchal society; they even reject the label 'feminism', since it implies a certain kind of essentialism. Postmodern feminism is aimed at highlighting the diversity, plurality and multiplicity of identity and existence. They challenge the assumptions and attitudes of Liberal and Radical feminists. Liberal feminists struggled for equality of opportunities, while Radical feminists identified patterns of discrimination and oppression against women in the analysis of assigned gender roles. Postmodern feminists are committed to the analysis of multiple points of view, in contrast to what they assume to be a predominantly white, male, bourgeois perspective. They find Radical feminists' approach towards the realities of gender oppression to be 'universalist'; for example, Shulamith Firestone finds biological differences to be the cause of rampant sexism in society. This approach suffers from the underlying inadequacy of being 'essentialising' and exclusionary of the diverse, fragmentary and contradictory ways in which gender oppression is related to other discourses of oppression.

Postmodernism, as an approach and theory, is received with certain scepticism and suspicion by feminists themselves. For instance, feminist writers such as Nancy Fraser and Linda J. Nicholson find Jean-François Lyotard's rejection of historical metanarratives problematic. Their argument is deduced from the fact that sexism is not ahistorical and is deeply entrenched and pervasive in every society. Thus, historical and sociological narratives need to be taken into account in feminist analyses.

Postmodern feminism aspires to be non-universalist and plural, challenging unitary notions of the woman and supplanting them with complex identities where gender is one of the elements, along with class, race, ethnicity, religion and sexual orientation. Postmodernism questions the existence of a coherent stable subject, thereby problematising and challenging traditional gender constructs. Postmodern feminists find the structuring of binary oppositions problematic. They find Radical feminists' celebration of 'difference' identical to Liberal feminists' emphasis on 'equality' or 'selfhood'. Both Liberal and Radical feminists, in their insistence on 'equality' and 'difference', erase the 'difference within' each category, by excluding categories of class, race, ethnicity and sexual preference.

As Judith Butler points out, in 'Gender Trouble, Feminist Theory and Psychoanalytic Discourse', 'If the inner truth of gender is a fabrication and if a true gender is a fantasy instituted and inscribed on the surface of bodies, then it seems that genders can be neither true nor false but are only produced as the truth effects of a discourse of primary and stable identity' (334). She argues that gender is a construct and a 'performance', rather than a biological fact. Butler's *Gender Trouble* questions the ideas of 'masculinity' and 'femininity'. Butler challenges the existence of a 'subject' and insists that it is a 'performative construct', while she differentiates between performance (which implies the presence of a subject) and performativity (which does not presuppose the presence of a subject). Drawing from de Beauvoir's claim that 'one is not born but becomes a woman', Butler argues in *Gender Trouble*, '. . . it follows that woman itself is a term in process, a becoming, a constructing, that cannot rightfully be said to originate or to end. As an ongoing discursive practice, it is open to intervention and resignification . . .' (33).

Western philosophy is historically aligned around the binaries of heterosexual normativity and biological determinism. Postmodern feminists contend that it is an 'essentialist' attitude to assume that gender and sex are fixed categories, since they are fluid and plural. They reject the dualistic view of gender as deterministic and flawed. The assumption that all women suffer oppression that is similar in nature is challenged by postmodern feminists. Critics such as Rosi Braidotti insist that no cognitive subject can avoid cultural conditionality and the acquisition of knowledge. Since there is only 'situated knowledge' (as theorised by Donna Haraway), women can no longer be understood as homogenous cognitive subjects. In the essay, 'Situated Knowledges: The Science Question in Feminism and the Privilege of Partial Perspective', Haraway had developed the idea of 'situated knowledge' in response to Sandra Harding's *The Science Question in Feminism*. 'Situated knowledge' is knowledge produced within a context, in which the ideals of objectivity are complicated and problematised by the context that produces the knowledge. This challenges the traditional masculinist view of objectivity that places the embodied ('marked') subjects (such as women, gay men, lesbian women, ethnic minorities, etc.) outside the scope of objectivity. 'Situated knowledge', in Haraway's definition, is localised, shared and connected, and is capable of forming a network of communities. Postmodern feminists question the possibility of objective and absolute knowledge and assert the importance of differences. Braidotti points out, 'By using the situatedness of each observer in a particular social, historical and political context, feminist post-modernists challenge the claim of any perspective on knowledge and reality to be impartial. . . . Feminist post-modernists stress plurality and difference' (45).

According to postmodern feminists, sex and gender cannot clearly be separated from each other. Here, we return to the ideas of Judith Butler. Butler insists that the binarisation of biological sex and the heterosexual norm derived from it should be viewed as a social construct. Gender is therefore what we 'do' rather than what we 'are'. Butler claims that gender is 'unnatural' since there cannot be any direct valence between one's body and one's gender, implying that having a woman's body does not presuppose the possession of 'feminine' traits. This idea of gender as delinked from biological sex makes it an incredibly unstable category, a 'free-floating artifice' as Butler claims. This, in turn, raises the question of understanding sex as a cultural construct as well. Butler argues that sex and gender categories are impositions that perpetuate heterosexuality as normative. Butler asserts that 'gender is not a noun (but it) proves to be performative, that is, constituting the identity it is purported to be. In this sense, gender is always a doing, though not doing by a subject who might be said to preexist the deed' (*Gender Trouble* 25). Using the logic that sex and gender are constructs and not 'natural' categories, Butler discusses the ideas of 'performativity' and 'parody'. In *Bodies That Matter* (1993), Butler suggests that sex does not exist before it is culturally inscribed. Like gender and sex, 'body' is also produced by discourses of 'science' and 'naturalness'. She questions the validity of ascribing 'naturalness' to the body: 'Is there a "physical" body prior to the perceptually perceived body? An impossible question to decide' (114). Butler collapses the sex/gender dichotomy and insists that there is no 'natural body' except in their gendered sense (as a consequence of socialisation). This leads to the deduction that gender is not something that 'is', rather, it is something that one 'does'. Butler emphasises that 'there is no gender identity behind the expression of gender; that identity is performatively constituted by the very "expressions" that are said to be its results' (*Gender Trouble* 25).

Postmodern feminism, thus, is an amalgamation of the strands of both postmodernism and feminism. It encompasses in its conceptual framework resistance to and rejection of universalist, essentialist notions of human nature, problematising the notion of the 'woman' and addressing the erasure of a multitude of differences. Postmodern feminists such as Fraser and Nicholson question the validity of a number of feminist theories (including those of Firestone, MacKinnon, Gilligan, Chodorow, etc.) for being quasi-metanarratives. Haraway attacks MacKinnon's theory as 'a caricature of the appropriating, incorporating, totalizing tendencies of western theories of identity grounding action' (200). She points out that in a culture of advanced technology, where the boundaries of man and animal, and animal and machine, are blurred, assigning gendered categories is problematic. She presents the instance of cyborgs, as a metaphor for Socialist feminism, since cyborgs elude the boundaries of hierarchical, gendered, normative, assigned categories. In 'A Manifesto for Cyborgs: Sciences, Technology and Socialist Feminism in the 1980s', Haraway presents the cyborg as a mythical symbol of postmodern feminism:

> Cyborg is a creature in a post-gender world; it has no truck with bisexuality, pre-Oedipal symbiosis, unalienated labour, or other seductions to organic wholeness through a final appropriation of all the powers of the parts into a higher unity ... the cyborg skips the step of original unity, of identification with nature in the Western sense. (192)

The idea of wholeness, which was an Enlightenment ideal, is exploded by this cyborg myth. In the figure of the cyborg, women can finally reconcile the rupture and fragmentation of the self/ other binary. The cyborgs blur the boundaries between human and machine, nature and nurture, man and woman. They offer a liberatory possibility for women, to destabilise and annul the paradigms of subjectivity and truth that have historically oppressed them. Haraway's theory does provide a framework of radical alterity, but it is riddled with the same anxieties and difficulties that postmodernism, as a phenomenon of a continuous sequence of fictionality and fragmentation, is informed with. Haraway's model offers a Utopian escape from the oppressive burden of the self/other dichotomy, but fails to address the necessity of a feminist politics based on agency and accountability.

POSTMODERNISM

The term postmodernism resists and disrupts all attempts to define it. The term was first coined by Arnold Toynbee in 1939; subsequently, it signified a complex, contradictory critical thought and aesthetic practice. The term came into use in the late 1970s, though the literary, cultural and artistic movements that are called 'postmodern' can be traced back to the 60s. Postmodernism has been variously interpreted as a particular kind of condition or cultural practice characterised by self-reflexivity, pastiche, parody, discontinuity and dispersal. The earliest usage of the term is found in Ihab Hassaan's 1971 seminal work *The Dismemberment of Orpheus: Toward a Postmodern Literature*. Postmodernism as a phenomenon and intellectual inquiry has challenged several assumptions and received ideas about culture, society, politics and philosophy. Influential postmodern theorists who have contributed in formulating various sets of principles to understand this essentially fragmented and frustratingly incomprehensible discourse are Jean-Francois Lyotard (1924–98), David Harvey (b.1935), Frederic Jameson (b.1934), Linda Hutcheon (b.1947), Jean Baudrillard (1929–2007), Yoshihiro Francis Fukuyama (b.1952) and Zygmunt Bauman (b.1925).

Metanarratives

A metanarrative is a set of rules that offers legitimacy to certain narratives. It implies a totalising, comprehensive grand narrative, or a narrative about narratives. Jean Francois Lyotard brought the term into prominence; he explains the postmodern condition as 'incredulity' towards metanarratives. It should not, however, be placed out of context to signify the rejection of all grand narratives, but understood as a feeling of scepticism about the legitimising discourse and the universalising rationalisations employed to establish metanarratives. Lyotard proposes that metanarratives should be replaced by *petit recits* – local, small narratives that address the heterogeneity of contemporary experience.

Jacques Marie Émile Lacan (1901–81)

Lacan is a profound influence on contemporary intellectual movements. His 'return to the meaning of Freud' contributed to the development of psychoanalysis, postmodernism, poststructuralism, feminism and film theory. Lacan emphasised the essentially divided nature of the subject and the importance of the unconscious. His article, 'The Mirror Stage as the Formative of the I', contributed to the poststructuralist thought that human identity is decentred. The registers of the Imaginary, the Symbolic and the Real are central to Lacanian psychoanalysis. Imaginary is the internalised image of the ideal, the whole self – it is the mediator of the external and the internal worlds. The symbolic stage is associated with language and is marked by the ways in which the subject is located in the plane which is loosely understood as 'reality'. 'Real' is pre-minor, pre-imaginary, pre-symbolic. Lacan's theory of subjectivity as being formed through language is hugely influential to feminist theory. Later, the French feminists rejected the phallocentrism of the Lacanaian model. Lacan's theory of femininity as a construct or category and woman as a social being, has opened new debates in feminism.

> ### JACQUES DERRIDA (1930–2004)
>
> Derrida, the eminent poststructuralist theorist, formulated 'deconstruction' as an interpretative strategy. His ideas have heavily influenced feminist theorists such as Luce Irigaray, Judith Butler and Gayatri Chakravorty Spivak. Derrida critiques logocentrism, the basis of Western metaphysical thought, which privileges speech over writing, in his works, *Of Grammatology* (1967), *Dissemination* (1972) and *Margins of Philosophy* (1972). He coined the term 'phallogocentrism' to point out the privileging of the masculine (phallus) over the feminine. He analyses sexual difference in *Glas* (1974) and *Spurs: Neitzsche's Styles* (1978), in which he emphasised the idea of sexuality beyond binary oppositions.

REFERENCES

Braidotti, Rosi. *Patterns of Dissonance*. New York: Routledge, 1991. Print.

Butler, Judith. *Gender Trouble and the Subversion of Identity*. New York: Routledge, 1990. Print.

---. 'Gender Trouble, Feminist Theory and Psychoanalytic Discourse.' *Feminism/Postmodernism*. Ed. Linda J. Nicholson. London: Routledge, 1990. 324–40. Print.

---. *Bodies That Matter*. New York: Routledge, 1993. Print.

Haraway, Donna. 'A Manifesto for Cyborgs: Sciences, Technology and Socialist Feminism in the 1980s.' *Feminism/Postmodernism*. Ed. Linda J. Nicholson. London: Routledge, 1990. 190–233. Print.

Owens, Craig. 'The Discourse of Others: Feminists and Postmodernism.' *Postmodern Culture*. Ed. Hal Foster. London: Pluto Press, 1985. 57–82. Print.

Chapter Six

L'écriture Féminine

KRISTEVA, CIXOUS, IRIGARAY

The French feminist group of Julia Kristeva (b.1941), Hélène Cixous (b.1937) and Luce Irigaray (b.1930) is deeply rooted in the tradition of philosophy and psychoanalysis, in their reconfiguration of the cultural understanding of 'femininity'. Their ideas came to be known among Anglo-American feminists only after 1979, with the publication of *New French Feminism* by Elaine Marks and Isabella de Courtivron. They interrogate, deconstruct and redefine the categories of subjectivity, identity, representation, aesthetics, sex and gender. While the Anglo-American tradition treats the 'other' as an extension of the 'self', thereby privileging patriarchal assumptions, the French feminists, on the other hand, delink the negative associations of 'feminine' attributes, such as formlessness, darkness and hysteria, and celebrate them. The Anglo-American feminists were concerned with the historicity of women's oppression and unearthing hitherto silenced women's voices. The French feminists, on the other hand, engaged with the theoretical paradigm, challenging Freudian, Lacanian and Derridean structures and drawing from them as well. They emphasise language as an essential agent for subverting patriarchal structures and empowering women. Feminist literary criticism was either concerned with exposing patriarchal representations of women or positing an alternative 'female-author' tradition. French feminism, on the contrary, engaged with reviewing and reconstructing the category of the 'feminine' in literature. They have, however, been accused of essentialism, ahistoricism and anti-empiricism, for centralising the female body in their theories of 'femininity' and 'feminine writing'. This group of French feminists mistrusts and challenges the system of binaries upheld by Liberal feminists. The traditional binaries of masculinity and femininity inherent in Western epistemology thrive on the deeply entrenched hierarchisation of the former over the latter. French feminists challenge the overt superiority that is assigned to men vis-à-vis women, adhering to the normative cultural constructions surrounding them. They emphasise the differences between the binaries rather than aspiring towards equality, in order to acknowledge the multiple subjectivities available to women. Kristeva, Irigaray and Cixous are reluctant to be labelled as 'feminists'; this reluctance emerges from their insistence on difference, which otherwise runs the risk of being subsumed in the legitimised patriarchal social systems and structures.

JULIA KRISTEVA

Kristeva occupies an ambivalent position with regard to feminist theory, since there are debates surrounding her contribution to it. She has been accused of being essentialist, anarchic, stereotypical, ahistorical and apolitical. The complicated relationship that Kristeva shares with feminism is largely due to the fact that she, like her Anglo-American counterparts, does argue in favour of subverting the conventional ways of discriminating against women; but unlike them, she does not subscribe to the view that men and women are alike. Kristeva advocates the 'third way' of feminism that can accommodate the 'spirit of adventure' as well as 'nest'. Toni Morrison, in an interview with Charles Ruas, states, 'The quality of nurturing is to me essential. . . . There should be a quality of adventure and a quality of nest' (qtd. in Taylor-Guthrie 104). This approach to feminism is situated both in the body and in the mind, in the biological plane as well as the intellectually creative sphere. According to Kristeva, these are not contradictory or mutually exclusive but can be brought together. Sex and gender, the representatives of biology and culture, cannot be sealed off from each other. They are interrelated and the differences between these categories are contextualised within the discourse of culture.

Kristeva underlines the importance of the body in feminist discourse with special focus on the maternal and pre-Oedipal states as stages in the construction of subjectivity. Anglo-American feminists cringe at centralising the feminine body in any feminist discussion, which they deem as biological essentialism and, as such, endangers their sense of autonomy. The distinction between sex and gender entails or fosters the binary between sexual-biological and cultural-linguistic. Kristeva's ideas of the 'semiotic' and the 'symbolic' do not adhere to such binaries; rather, there is simultaneity in these two states in the discourse of the speaking subject. Kristeva insists that all signification is composed of 'semiotic' and 'symbolic' components. The 'semiotic' is that element of the signifying process that comprises the bodily drives discharged in representation. This process is linked with the rhythm and tone that is essentially related to the maternal body, thereby establishing a connection between the semiotic and the maternal body. The semiotic, for Kristeva, is that subterranean element of the signifying process that 'Freudian psychoanalysis points to in postulating not only the *facilitation* and the structuring *disposition* of drives, but also the so-called primary processes which displace and condense both energies and their inscription' (Moi 93). Kristeva uses the term 'chora' in concurrence with 'semiotic'. The 'chora' is a 'rhythmic space, which has no thesis and no position, the process by which significance is constituted' (Kristeva, *Revolution in Poetic Language* 26). The 'symbolic' is the grammar and structure of signification; it is that stage where language is orderly and logical. Kristeva argues that these two are interdependent – without the symbolic, all utterances would be delirium; but without the semiotic, signification would be vacuous. Thus signification requires both.

Kristeva asserts that there is a 'maternal regulation' or law presaging the paternal law. In fact, she underscored the indispensability of the maternal function in the development of subjectivity. Freud and Lacan held that a child enters the social discourse by paternal law, driven by fears of castration. Kristeva challenges this assumption in 'Tales of Love'; she interrogates the rationale of the child's desire to leave the safe haven of the maternal body, if only fear and threats await him. In 'Powers of Horror', Kristeva develops the notion of 'abjection', which is necessary to understand the systems of oppression. Abjection is that process of the psyche by which the subjective and group identity is consolidated by excluding those elements which threaten one's own or the group's autonomy. In patriarchal cultures, the maternal body is abjected; but women cannot abject the maternal body because as women they identify themselves with the body of the mother. Kristeva accounts for women's oppression and degradation in patriarchal cultures with the misplaced abjection of women, maternity and maternal function.

One of the inherent problems of feminist philosophy is its inability to assign a fixed definition for the category 'woman' without any reference to her difference. In an attempt to elude this problem, Kristeva, in 'Stabat Mater' (1977), seeks to analyse maternity as a trope that is always associated with women. Here, Kristeva moves between two registers and modes of expression. While the primary text recounts the mythology of the Virgin Mary, the text in the margin conveys a visceral expression of Kristeva's own experiences during pregnancy:

> One does not give birth in pain, one gives birth to pain: the child represents it and henceforth it settles in, it is continuous. Obviously you may close your eyes, cover up your ears, teach courses, run errands, tidy up the house, think about objects, subjects. But a mother is always branded by pain, she yields to it. (167)

The boundaries between the 'self' and the 'other' are blurred in the act of giving birth. The child is physically detached from the mother and is thus the 'other', yet it derives life from the mother. Thus, maternity is, in the Kristevan paradigm, 'radical alterity within identity' (Oliver 105). This entails the representation of the mother as a 'subject-in-process', the 'self' that contains the 'other' within it. The myth of the Virgin Mary, Kristeva says, is symbolic of a fantasy of Western culture, predominantly patriarchal, of a maternal love that is representative of self-abnegation and asceticism. Western culture equates motherhood with femininity; this misleads feminists into discarding motherhood by which they hope to discard the stereotypes of femininity. This misplaced abjection is what Kristeva finds responsible for women's oppression. She formulates an ethics that defies both matriarchal and patriarchal laws. She aspires towards a *herethics*, or 'the heretical ethics of love', which would not require women to either conform to restrictive patterns or become absolute anarchists. Kristeva suggests a strategy by which women can establish their identity without renouncing their difference.

In 'Black Sun', Kristeva argues that not only a new discourse of maternity but also a new discourse of the relationship between the mother and the daughter is needed. In 'Women's Time', Kristeva explores the three phases of feminism. However, she does not use a generation or a phase of feminism in its conventional sense but to imply 'a signifying space, a both corporeal and desiring mental space' (213). She rejects the first phase of feminism as it advocates universal equality and overlooks sexual difference. The first generation of feminists attempted to locate women within the scope of linear history, which was previously a masculine domain. This, Kristeva argues, tends to reject the particularity or differences among women by employing a universalist and essentialising pattern. She even critiques Simone de Beauvoir's rejection of motherhood; rather, Kristeva argues for a new discourse for maternity. In 'A New Type of Intellectual: The Dissident', Kristeva suggests that 'real female innovation (in whatever field) will only come about when maternity, female creation and the links between them are better understood' (298). She rejects the second phase of feminism as well, since it seeks a uniquely feminine language. She does not adhere to the view which insists upon abandoning language and culture, as they are understood to be patriarchal. Rather, for Kristeva, language and culture fall under the realm of 'speaking beings' and women are inherently speaking beings. The second phase of feminism moves away from the first generation's insistence on the equality of the sexes, but their revolt against the established order is often violent and sexist. She endorses the third phase of feminism which seeks to establish an interface between identity and difference without privileging either. The third generation does not supplant or succeed the previous two generations but is related to them. The focus of the new generation of feminists would be to '. . . combine the sexual with the symbolic in order to discover first the specificity of the feminine and then the specificity of each woman' ('Women's Time' 210). The third generation of feminists, Kristeva hopes, would dismantle the monolithic category of 'woman' and address individual and particular differences.

Kristeva is against any fixed idea of 'feminine essence' which often overruns individual differences among women. She is rather sceptical about that politics of feminism which adheres to a group identity of 'women'. She acknowledges it as an important agency for the politics of empowerment, but it also runs the risk of being counter-discursive. Feminism, Kristeva believes, should outgrow its 'herd' mentality and address individual differences, especially sexual differences.

HÉLÈNE CIXOUS

Like Kristeva and Irigaray, Cixous too engages with Derridian deconstruction and Lacanian psychoanalysis in her radical postulations on women's creative expression. She, however, disclaims the tag of being a feminist, since she identifies the 'feminist' movement as an attempt on the part of women to duplicate the same patriarchal structure and quest for phallocentrism. She was initially involved with the controversial group 'Psych et Po' ('Psychanalyse et Politique') but later moved away from it. Between 1976 and 1982, Cixous published all her work with *Des Femmes*, the publishing house of this group. Apart from being a theorist, Cixous is also a renowned creative writer. Her *Le Prenom de Dieu* (1967) is a collection of short stories; her autobiographical fiction, *Dedans* (1969), won the Prix Medices Award. She, however, privileges poetry as the expression of the unconscious and invests it with considerable power.

Cixous's influential essays, 'The Laugh of the Medusa' (1975) and 'Sorties' (1975), expose patriarchal orthodoxies while exploring the interrelation between women's desire and women's language. She challenges the general tendency of categorising gender identities into binaries and in the process privileging phallogocentrism over femininity. The binaries constructed are: activity/passivity, sun/moon, nature/culture, day/night, father/mother. There is an inherent privileging of one category over the other, a destruction of one category for the establishment of the other. In this patterning, the female is always relegated to the space of the 'other'. In 'Castration and Decapitation', Cixous insists,

> Man/Woman automatically means great/small, superior/inferior ... means high or low, means Nature/History, means transformation/inertia. In fact every theory of the culture, every theory of society, the whole conglomeration of symbolic system – everything that is, that's spoken, everything that's organized as discourse, art, religion, the family, language, everything that seizes us, everything that acts us – it is all ordered around hierarchical opposition that come back to man/woman oppositions. (279)

In 'The Laugh of the Medusa', Cixous asserts *'l'écriture féminine'* as a counter-practice in writing to challenge and subvert the masculinist/phallogocentric notion of subjectivity. She rejects the binaries of masculinity and femininity and insists on bisexuality as a marker of plurality. It subverts fixed gender identities and opens up plural libidinal possibilities. This, however, is not restricted to one gender, despite its overt labelling of the 'feminine'. The sex of the author is irrelevant, what is important is the kind of writing he or she practises. Cixous, however, identifies a significant link between bisexuality and women's experience, which leads her to the assumption that this kind of writing would be predominantly women's writing: 'By writing her self, woman will return to the body which has been more than confiscated from her, which has been turned into the uncanny stranger on display – the ailing or dead figure, which so often turns out to be the nasty companion, the cause and location of inhibitions' (261–62). *L'écriture féminine* challenges the systematic oppression of women's experiences by the masculinist, phallocentric discourse of Western thought. It sets out to overthrow patriarchal structures fuelled by the conviction that women's psyche is different from men's. Cixous employs the psychoanalytic and poststructuralist frameworks of Lacan, Barthes and Derrida, but critiques their theories as well. The concept of 'jouissance' is given a feminine specificity. Barthes' idea of 'the pleasure of the text' is reworked to establish an anti-patriarchal, anti-phallic, feminine writing, which finds pleasure from not just the text, but also from the source of the text, that is, the woman's own body. The female body is central to Cixous's proposed subversive writing strategy. She urges women to discover and articulate their libidinal impulses in order to triumph over the repressive instincts indoctrinated in them. Women's libido is differently realised and expressed: 'A woman's body with its thousand and one thresholds of ardour – once, by smashing yokes and censors, she lets it articulate the profusion of meanings that run through it in every direction – will make the old single-grooved mother tongue reverberate with more than one language' (Cixous, 'The Laugh of the Medusa' 267). In fact, she makes Dora, the hysterical patient of Freud, the 'speaking subject' in *Portrait de Dora* (1975), a representative, rebel figure, who subverts the established system.

In 'The Laugh of the Medusa', Medusa is a beautiful, laughing woman who debunks Freudian ideas of castration. In the essay, Cixous celebrates the female body and rejects the Freudian and Lacanian perception of the woman as 'lack'. In 'Sorties', Cixous expresses her concern over the fact that women often – swayed by the belief that maternity is allied to the exploitative structure of capitalism – repress other women who desire to have children. She identifies maternity as a drive, equivalent to writing, that signifies the immense possibilities for women to articulate their subjectivities. Like Irigaray and Kristeva, Cixous underlines the significance of the mother-daughter relationship in women's speech and writing. In fact, she exhorts feminine writing to be linked to the 'white ink' of the mother's milk. Women's writing is not comparable to men's writing on any level, since it articulates an entirely different bodily experience. In 'The Laugh of the Medusa', Cixous underlines that '. . . she physically materializes what she's thinking; she signifies it with her body. In a certain way she inscribes what she's saying' (263).

Cixous decentres attention from the sex of the author to the expression of female sexuality and desire in the text. Masculine and feminine are attributes that are traditionally assigned to one sex or another. Feminine writing can be produced by both men and women. This belief is driven by the assumption that all human beings are inherently bisexual. The creative artist must contain both the positions, of male and female, within her/himself. According to Cixous, since women occupy a marginal position, she is more prone to bisexuality. Cixous's understanding of 'difference' is complex since she refers to the possibility of a multiplicity of differences within subjects. Language can become a tool in women's hands to assert and empower themselves. By using language according to their desire, women can dismantle the monolithic, unitarian discourse promoted by the masculinist perspective.

In 'Allerà la mer' (1977), published in *Le Monde*, Cixous puts forward her manifesto for drama. She aspires for a theatre where 'woman is whole, where instead of being acted out, life is lived'. She insists that, 'it is high time that women gave back to the theatre its fortunate position, its *raison d'etre* and what makes it different – the fact that there it is possible to get across the living, breathing, speaking body' (134).

LUCE IRIGARAY

Irigaray reviews philosophy, psychoanalysis and linguistics to propound an influential feminist philosophy. From her first book, *Speculum of the Other Woman* (1974), onwards Irigaray has exposed the fact that philosophers from Plato to Freud have excluded women from subject positions. While maternal properties have been traditionally associated with nature and 'unthinking' matter, men on the contrary, occupy the central role in the realms of culture and subjectivity. Irigaray points out the irony wherein women are relegated to the 'other' position, yet are indispensable to the advancement of society. Irigaray goes on to claim that Western culture is founded on the sacrifice of the mother and all women by extension.

In *Speculum of the Other Woman*, Irigaray unearths the reality that epistemological, ontological and metaphysical truths are constructed from a male perspective, while women are denigrated as insignificant matters. Irigaray argues that both men and women need to reposition their subjectivities, so that they straddle both nature and culture. This change can be effected, in Irigaray's analysis, in the development of the female imaginary. This would result in the transformation of the symbolic order and help women achieve subjectivities. She articulates female ontology differently: 'woman,' she insists, is 'neither open nor closed. She is indefinite, in-finite, *form is never complete in her*. . . . (The/a) woman refers to what cannot be defined, enumerated, formulated or formalized' (229–30 ; emphasis in the original).

In *An Ethics of Sexual Difference*, Irigaray asserts that the differences between the sexes are not anatomical but located in language. She subscribes to the Lacanian view of the ego formation in the Symbolic order. In 'The Mirror Stage as Formative of the I', Lacan provides a theory about bodily ego or imaginary anatomy. According to this, the understanding of one's body is interrelated with language and image-formation in the mirror stage. This is further complicated by the subject's entry into the Symbolic order. Irigaray accedes to the Lacanian concept of the imaginary body being influenced by culture. However, she extends her argument by stating that this culture-induced imaginary body is fundamentally against women. According to Irigaray's thesis, in Western monosexual culture, the male body is the imaginary body since it privileges identity, unity, autonomy, and all those attributes which are culturally and conventionally assigned to the male anatomy. In *This Sex which is Not One* (1977), Irigaray is sceptical of the Lacanian insistence that the phallus, as the signifier of the Symbolic order, is ahistorical. This, in fact, is a projection of the male anatomy, a defective signifier of the Symbolic order, thus specifically biased against women. Another key element in which Irigaray differs from the Lacan is in her conviction that the language system is malleable and therefore subject to the power relationship in a state of flux.

In her major works, Irigaray exposes the exclusion of all things feminine in philosophers such as Aristotle, Decartes, Kant and Hegel. She is influenced by several philosophers, but her enterprise of creating and redefining women as a category precludes privileging any particular philosophy. The history of Western discourse has relegated women to the negative side of the masculine or merely as complementary to it. From Plato to Hegel, she observes, masculinity remains the subject of knowledge, while Reason is privileged over all else. The female body, female sexuality and female subjectivity are constituted by and in the masculinist paradigm. The Cartesian model views the subject as *res cogitans*, or the thinking subject, while the rest fall under the purview of *res extensa,* or the extended substance. Since the subject position is occupied by the masculine principle, women are relegated to the extended substance, or the 'unthinking' substance. The feminists' attempt to bring women to a position of equality, in Irigaray's analysis, is counterproductive, since it relinquishes the specific relationship that women share with the Imaginary; at the same time, it fails to transform the patriarchal Symbolic order. She underscores the necessity of a specific female language, '*la parler femme*', which is ideologically capable of disrupting the phallocentric order:

> [masculine] domination of the philosophical logos stems in large part from its power to reduce all others to the economy of the Same: [...] Whence the necessity of 're-opening' the figures of philosophical discourse – idea, substance, transcendental subjectivity, absolute knowledge – in order to pry out of them what they have borrowed that is feminine, from the feminine, to make them 'render up' and give back what they owe the feminine. (*This Sex which is Not One* 74)

Irigaray insists that mimicry/masquerade can be an act of resisting traditional feminine roles. It is a strategy of playing within the same stereotypes of femininity in order to interrogate them:

> To play with mimesis is thus, for a woman, to try to recover the place of her exploitation by discourse, without allowing herself to be simply reduced to it. It means to resubmit herself – in as much as she is on the side of the 'perceptible', of 'matter' – to 'ideas', in particular to ideas about herself, that are elaborated in/by a masculine logic, but so as to make 'visible', by an effect of playful repetition, what was supposed to remain invisible: the cover up of a possible operation of the feminine in language. (*The Sex which is Not One* 76)

The negative views associated with femininity can be discarded if these are subjected to playful, subversive demystification. For example, if women's bodies are understood to be dispersed, fragmented, women must speak from that position in order to underpin the fact that these are patriarchal assumptions. The purpose is to challenge the established definitions of women and to reconfigure new definitions for the subject positions that women can occupy. This, Irigaray insists, has to be done by/in a collective endeavour. She advocates the reviewing of the mother-daughter relationship in which mothers should represent themselves differently to their daughters. Like Kristeva and Cixous, Irigaray refuses to be associated with any particular group of feminist movement. Organisations and outfits can adversely affect the solidarity of women in the dismantling of patriarchal structures. She is particularly involved in the Italian feminist movement. Many of her works – *I Love to You: Sketch of a Possible Felicity within History* (1990), *Democracy Begins between Two* (1994) and *Two be Two* (1997) – are occasioned by her participation in the Italian women's movement.

The French feminists challenged several assumptions of Anglo-American feminism. They were considerably influenced by poststructuralism and psychoanalysis in the way they radicalised the traditional binarisms inherent in Western epistemology. In the 1970s, there was a political exuberance in France, stimulating the women's movement as well, which coalesced into the *Movement de Liberation des Femmes* (MLF). Cixous and Kristeva have, however, been sceptical about the label 'feminism'; nonetheless, they have assigned a particular value to their situation as women. Another important moment in French feminism was the establishment of the journal *Question Feminist* in 1977.

French feminism explored the implications of such categories as identity, sex and gender from the female perspective, valorising the same attributes that were employed for 'othering' women. French feminism reviewed the functions of language, the role of the unconscious and the legitimacy of epistemological boundaries.

> **SHORT TAKES**
>
> ### Freud: Id, Ego, Superego
>
> Sigmund Freud (1865–1939) offered a tripartite model of subjectivity – Id, Ego and Superego. Id is the innate instinctual self; Superego is the self that has internalised cultural norms; Ego is the mediating self between Id and Superego. Freud's ideas of the Oedipus complex and 'penis envy' have been severely challenged by feminist theorists.

REFERENCES

Cixous, Helene. 'Aller à la mer.' *Twentieth Century Theatre: A Sourcebook*. Ed. Richard Drain. New York: Routledge, 1995. 133–35. Print.
---. 'Castration and Decapitation.' *French Feminism Reader*. Ed. Kelly Oliver. Maryland: Rowman and Littlefield Publishers, 2000. 276–90. Print.
---. 'The Laugh of the Medusa.' *French Feminism Reader*. Ed. Kelly Oliver. Maryland: Rowman and Littlefield Publishers, 2000. 257–75. Print.
Irigaray, Luce. *Speculum of the Other Woman*. Trans. Gillian C. Gill. Ithaca: Cornell UP, 1985. Print.
---. *This Sex which is Not One*. Trans. Catherine Porter. New York: Cornell UP, 1985. Print.
Kristeva, Julia. *Revolution in Poetic Language*. Trans. Leon S. Roudiez. New York: Columbia UP, 1984. Print.
---. 'Stabat Mater.' *The Kristeva Reader*. Ed. Toril Moi. New York: Columbia UP, 1986. 160–86. Print.
---. 'Women's Time.' *The Kristeva Reader*. Ed. Toril Moi. New York: Columbia UP, 1986. 187–213. Print.
---. 'A New Type of Intellectual: The Dissident.' *The Kristeva Reader*. Ed. Toril Moi. New York: Columbia UP, 1986. 292–300, Print.
Moi, Toril. *Sexual/Textual Politics: Feminist Literary Theory*. New York: Routledge, 1986. Print.
Oliver, Kelly. 'Julia Kristeva's Feminist Revolutions.' *Hypatia* 8.3 (Summer 1993). Web. 11 November 2014. <http://www.jstor.org/stable/3810407>.
Taylor-Guthrie, Danille, ed. *Conversations with Toni Morrison*. Jackson: U of Mississippi P, 1994. Print.

Chapter Seven

Black Feminism

The equality-difference debate, which is central to feminism, assumes greater significance in relation to race, class, sexuality and ability. Mainstream feminists have often been accused of obscuring these differences in their tendency to universalise their analyses and resolutions of the oppression of women. The heterogeneity of feminism, in approach, attitude and practice, compels an interrogation into the generalising tendencies of the first- and second-wave feminisms. These movements were dominated by white, middle-class women who overlooked the concerns and experiences of working-class and black women. Black feminism emerged as a challenge to the assumptions made by these white feminists regarding their prerogative to speak for all women in general. Black feminism insists that sexism and racism are imbricated in each other; the oppression of women cannot be understood and addressed without reference to racism. They mistrusted the white feminist's stronghold over feminism as theory and practice, underpinning the sticky issue of the white feminist's tendency to treat black feminism as the 'other'. Black feminism demands an acknowledgement of the diversity in feminist concerns, while they confront the stereotypes imposed on them, not only by white people but also by black men. According to Claudia Jones, a Trinidad-born activist,

> In the film, radio and press, the Negro woman is not pictured in her real role as bread winner, mother and protector of the family, but as a traditional 'mammy' who puts the care of

children and families of others above her own. This traditional stereotype of the Negro Slave mother, which to this day appears in commercial advertisements, must be combated and rejected as a device of the imperialist to perpetuate that white chauvinist ideology that Negro women are 'backward' 'inferior' and the 'natural slaves of others'. (qtd. in Jarrett-Macauley x)

Black feminism emerged out of a history of activism, engaged in by Maria Stewart (1803–80), Harriet Tubman (1822–1913), Sojourner Truth (1797–1883), Rosa Parks (1913–2005), etc. Although women of colour had participated in the suffrage movement and strove to expose the linkage between racism and sexism as the means of white male dominance, first-wave feminism remained the domain of white, middle-class, educated women. The cult of true womanhood remained hinged on the image of women as delicate, fragile, dependent, docile and homely. The material lives of African-American women as workers outside homes, condemned to be a subhuman inferior species, complicate the construction of gender empowerment by Euro-centric models. Sojourner Truth delivered a forceful speech, 'Ain't I a Woman?', in the Women's Convention held in Ohio in 1851, underscoring her 'difference' as an ex-slave black woman and contradicting the model of gender in which Euro-American women were both incarcerated and nurtured:

> Nobody ever helps me into carriage, or over mud-puddles, or gives me any best place! And ain't I a woman? Look at me! Look at my arm! I have ploughed and planted, and gathered into barns, and no man could head me! And ain't I a woman? . . . I have borne thirteen children and seen most all sold off to slavery, and when I cried out with my mother's grief, none but Jesus heard me! And ain't I a woman? (Web n.p.)

In the 1960s and 70s, the black feminist movement emerged from the discontent with the Civil Rights movement as well as the white feminist movement. In *All the Women are White, All the Blacks are Men but Some of Us are Brave*, Gloria Hull, Patricia Bell Scott and Barbara Smith explore the intersectionality of black women in the discourse of the Civil Rights movement and the contemporary feminist movement. While the former primarily addressed the oppression of black men, the latter focused on the problems that were specific to white women. The agenda of black feminists was to establish their identity against patriarchy in their culture, and the models established by the mainstream feminists. The NBFO (National Black Feminist Organization) was established in 1973, and the Combahee River Collective, a black, lesbian, socialist, feminist outfit, was founded by Barbara Smith in 1974. They were directed towards addressing the issues of race and gender which were central to the development of a black feminist consciousness. In 1970, the Third World Women's Alliance published the *Black Women's Manifesto*, which emphasised the distinctiveness of the oppression that black women faced. The manifesto advocated the dismantling of conventional stereotypes assigned to the black woman and acknowledged her distinct identity.

Black feminist criticism challenges the narrow boundaries of the experiential visions as well as the traditional Western models of theory-building. It steers clear of the 'race for theory' and is moored in practice, as 'experience' is central to the analysis of the history and culture of African-American women's lives. As bell hooks (Gloria Jean Watkins), the feminist activist and academic, points out, black feminist criticism attempts to extend the dialogue about the nature of black women's experience that began in nineteenth-century America, to move beyond racist and sexist assumptions about the nature of black womanhood. Social scientists such as Patricia Hill Collins, the author of *Black Feminist Thought: Knowledge, Consciousness and the Politics of Empowerment* (1990), insist that experience is crucial in understanding and critiquing the lives of the 'raced women'. Thus, the analysis, as a part of the black feminist project, needed to be predicated on the everyday lives of African-American women. Smith finds the politics of race and the politics of sex interlocked in the works of black women writers. In 'Towards a Black Feminist Criticism', she stresses the necessity of a combination of black feminist criticism and black feminist political movement. Her approach is a radical departure from such earlier works as Mary Helen Washington's *Black-Eyed Susans*. Washington was less concerned with providing any black feminist critical perspective but concentrated on the reconnaissance of obscure and neglected texts by black women writers. Smith, however, laid down certain parameters to evaluate such works:

> The use of Black women's language and cultural experiences in books by Black women about Black women results in a miraculously rich coalescing of form and content and also takes their writing far beyond the confines of white/male literary structures. The Black feminist critic would find innumerable commonalities in works by Black women. (417)

Hazel Carby, in *Reconstructing Womanhood: The Emergence of the Afro-American Woman Novelist*, revises some of the previous structures established by the forerunners of black feminist criticism, and interrogates the essentialising assumptions made about black feminism. She highlights the underlying racism in the Suffrage and Temperance movements and analyses the works of black women writers as cultural and political documents forming an intellectual tradition. She also provides an interesting exposition on the revolutionary, subversive potential of women Blues artists. She concurs that racism and sexism are interlocked, but emphasises the importance of establishing historically specific forms of this interface: '. . . racisms and sexisms need to be regarded as particular historical practices articulated with each other and with other practices in social formation' (18).

Valerie Smith, in 'Black Feminist Theory and the Representation of the Other', points out the necessity of destabilising the centrality or privileging of one category over the other, as practised by Anglo-American feminists and male African-American critics. Smith argues in favour of a flexible and shifting perspective on otherness for black feminists:

> I understand the phrase black feminist theory to refer not only to theory written (or practiced) by black feminists, but also to a way of reading inscriptions of race (particularly but not exclusively blackness), gender (particularly but not exclusively womanhood), and class in modes of cultural expressions. (312)

Smith identifies the 'archaeological projects' that form the first stage of black feminist criticism. Works such as Toni Cade Bambara's *The Black Woman: An Anthology*, Washington's *Black-Eyed Susans: Classic Stories by and about Black Women*, and Mari Evans's *Black Women Writers*

(1950–1980) fall under this category. The republication of primary texts is a significant contribution to the 'archaeological' project – these include, Henry Louis Gates's 1982 edition of Harriet Wilson's *Our Nig* (first published in 1859) and Jean Fagan Yellin's edition of Harriet Jacob's *Incidents in the Life of a Slave Girl* (first published in 1861). This stage was followed by the stage of textual analysis of the works of black women writers, underscoring their engagement with diverse significant issues such as marginalisation, otherness, sexuality, identity-formation, hegemony and counter-discourse, and community life. Interventions by mainstream theoretical perspectives such as psychoanalysis (as in the works of the critic, Hortense Spillers) and reader-response theory (by theorists such as Debora McDowell) supplement the project of textual analysis.

Black women writers such as Toni Morrison, Alice Walker, Gwendolyn Brooks and Maya Angelou have effectively represented black women at the centre of highly contested ideologies of race, class and gender. Marginality as an agency of resistance (and repression) is an iterative theme in the works of bell hooks. In *Ain't I a Woman: Black Women and Feminism* and *Feminist Theory: From Margin to Center*, hooks is forceful in her condemnation of racism, classism and sexism, while analysing popular culture and consumerism. Though they are not wholly convinced by the idea of 'sisterhood' forwarded by some white feminists, black feminists, however, do not advocate separatism. As Audre Lorde points out, 'By and large . . . , white women focus upon their oppression as women and ignore the differences of race, sexual preference, class and age. There is a pretense to homogeneity of experience covered by the word sisterhood that does not in fact exist' (282).

Alice Walker, in her Preface to *In Search of Our Mothers' Gardens*, introduces the idea of the 'womanist', which is to feminist as 'purple to lavender'. This is not simply an oppositional position to feminism *per se*, but an inclusive strategy of acknowledging black women's strength, their survival skills and vitality. It, however, does not preclude men; they are an integral part of a black woman's life as her children, husband or lover. 'Womanism' is committed to the 'survival and wholeness of an entire people, male and female'(xi), celebrating the multiple ways in which women overcome oppression and exploitation. Walker underlines the presence of matrilineage in female creativity; the stories, gardens, quilts and other creations by black female artists bear traces of the experiences and traditions of their mothers and grandmothers who were deprived of creative expression by the historical circumstances of oppression and dehumanisation. Traditionally, the family has been regarded as a site for discrimination against women, but for black women, the family can be a site of resistance and agency. This is mainly because women are often the sole breadwinners in black families, thereby enjoying a degree of autonomy not experienced by their white counterparts.

The universalist models of feminist struggle and strategies are not always valid for black women's experiences and realities. For instance, Angela Davis, in *Women, Race and Class*, has exposed the discrimination in the compulsory sterilisation programme inflicted on the coloured women in the 1970s, while the white women aborted children due to unplanned pregnancies:

> The abortion rights activists of the early 1970s should have examined the history of their movement.... They might have understood how important it was to undo the racist deeds of their predecessors, who had advocated birth control as well as compulsory sterilization as a means of eliminating the 'unfit' sectors of the population. (361)

The community plays a major role in the black woman's experience as is manifest in her literature. Stanlie James refers to the unique practice of 'other mothering', in which nurturing and caring activities, usually associated with biological mothering, are transformed into larger social practices with socio-political implications. It engages nurturing as a vital means of addressing specific needs resulting from concrete social, political and economic inequities (51).

It is, however, undeniable that black feminism has, to a considerable degree, succeeded in subverting hierarchies and dismantling stereotypes, but it still remains a site of conflicts between ideal models and real social conditions. Black womanhood is infused with a unique consciousness of a 'double bind', of oppression and liberation, but also occupies the intersectional position between race, class and gender conflicts.

> ### CIVIL RIGHTS MOVEMENT
>
> The Civil Rights Movement of the 1960s raised important questions about problems of inequality. It was a mass protest against racial segregation that had its roots in the institutions of slavery in America. Though slavery was abolished, slaves were freed as a result of the Civil War, and civil rights were granted through the Fourteenth and Fifteenth Amendments of the US constitution, blacks never really received the benefits. Black Americans in the South were denied the right to vote, segregated from public facilities, exploited and abused. In the North too, blacks faced discrimination, disenfranchisement and subordination. Despite the fact that the Supreme Court had ruled in favour of desegregation in public schools in the Brown vs Board of Education Case, black Americans were denied adequate access to educational institutions. Martin Luther King Jr emerged as an iconic figure in the Civil Rights Movement, leading non-violent protests to end segregation and discrimination against blacks. The Civil Rights Act, passed on 3 July 1964, was foundational in ensuring full legal equality and citizenship for black Americans.

> ### HARLEM RENAISSANCE
>
> The Harlem Renaissance of the 1920s is probably the most influential movement in the African-American literary tradition. The movement engaged visual arts, music, theatre and literature, in redefining the 'negro' stereotype delinked from its negative connotations assigned by the white hegemonic discourse. It was triggered by the Great Migration from the South to the various settlements of the North. The Harlem district of New York was the epicentre of this intellectual and creative movement, but it was widespread in its influence. The important figures of the movement included W. E. B. Dubois, Langston Hughes, Alain Locke, James Baldwin and Zora Neale Hurston.

> **SHORT TAKES**
>
> **INTERSECTIONALITY**
>
> Kimberlé Williams Crenshaw coined the term 'intersectionality' in her 1989 essay, 'Demarginalising the Intersection of Race and Sex: A Black Feminist Critique of Antidiscrimination Doctrine, Feminist Theory and Antiracist Poetics'. She argues that black women are marginalised not by racism or sexism separately but by an intersection of racism and sexism. The legal framework makes black women 'invisible' since they do not address this intersectionality of discrimination. This concept echoes the point made by Sojourner Truth in her speech 'Ain't I a Woman'. Patricia Hill Collins, in her *Black Feminist Thought: Women, Knowledge, Consciousness and the Politics of Empowerment* (1990), uses the same paradigm of intersectionality to focus on the multiple oppressions experienced by black women.

REFERENCES

Carby, Hazel. *Reconstructing Womanhood: The Emergence of the Afro-American Woman Novelist*. New York: Oxford UP, 1987. Print.

Davis, Angela. 'Racism, Birth Control and Reproductive Rights.' *Feminist Postcolonial Theory: A Reader*. Ed. Reina Lewis and Sara Mills. New York: Routledge, 2003. 353–67. Print.

James, Stanlie. 'Mothering: A Possible Black Feminist Link to Social Transformation?' *Theorizing Black Feminism: The Visionary Pragmatism of Black Women*. Ed. Stanlie James and A. P. Busia. London: Routledge, 1999. 44–54. Print.

Lorde, Audre. 'Age, Race, Class and Sex: Women Redefining Difference.' *Out There: Marginalization and Contemporary Culture*. Ed. Russel Ferguson et al. Massachusetts: MIT Press, 1990. 281–87. Print.

Jarrett-Macauley, Delia, ed. *Reconstructing Womanhood, Reconstructing Feminism: Writings on Black Women*. London: Routledge, 1996. Print.

Smith, Barbara. 'Towards a Black Feminist Criticism.' *Within the Circle: An Anthology of African American Literary Criticism from the Harlem Renaissance to the Present*. Ed. Angelyn Mitchell. North Carolina: Duke UP, 1994. 410–27. Print.

Smith, Valerie. 'Black Feminist Theory and the Representation of the "Other".' *Feminisms: An Anthology of Literary Theory and Criticism.* Ed. Robyn R. Warhol and Diane Price Herndl. New Jersey: Rutgers UP, 1997. 311–25. Print.

Truth, Sojourner. 'Ain't I a Woman?' Web. 14 November 2014. <http://www.fordham.edu/halsall/mod/sojtruth-woman.asp>.

Walker, Alice. *In Search of Our Mothers' Gardens: Womanist Prose.* California: Harcourt, 1983.

Chapter Eight
Postcolonial Feminism and Third World Feminism

Postcolonial feminist theory intends to address the issues that have not been explored in mainstream postcolonial theory and Western feminism. It marks a shift, a movement away, from the concerns of white, middle-class, educated, English-speaking women and engages with issues related to women from diverse national and cultural contexts. This 'worlding' (Mills 98) of feminist theory also questions the authority and authenticity of the white feminist's claims of representing or 'speaking for' all women. It has also occasioned a reconfiguration of postcolonial theory with reference to the gender question. Postcolonial feminism has, in the process, come into its own, not only as an oppositional approach to mainstream feminism or postcolonialism but as a distinct system of ideas and attitudes. Postcolonial feminism is aimed at theorising the differences and diversities of the 'other' women against the Western feminist's tendency to universalise women's oppression.

Gayatri Chakravorty Spivak underlines the importance of the material histories and lives of 'Third World' women in understanding the heterogeneity of oppression and women's struggles against it. This broadens the purview of contemporary feminist discourse. In her essays, 'French Feminism in an International Frame' (1981) and 'Feminism and Critical Theory' (1986), Spivak not only provides pertinent commentary on, but also critiques, the theories of French feminists such as Julia Kristeva, Luce Irigaray and Hélène

Cixous. Patriarchy – in collaboration with other oppressive agencies such as the church, other religious institutions and the law – tends to project/establish a binary structure, which historically and ideologically subordinates women. Spivak proposes a counter-strategy which imitates the negative stereotypical representations of women, the subaltern or the working class. She calls this 'strategic essentialism'. Spivak's major contribution to the feminist debate on essentialism is in shifting the focus from the issue of sexual difference to the reality of cultural difference between the women of the 'Third World' and those of the 'First World'. In 'French Feminism in an International Frame', she rejects the tendency of Western feminists to intervene in/interpret the experiences of 'Third World' women from their subject position. She gives the instance of Mahasweta Devi's 'Breast Giver' where Jashoda, an impoverished subaltern woman, works as a professional wet nurse to nourish the children of an upper-class Brahmin family in order to sustain her crippled husband Kangali. Her breast milk and reproductive body are exploited, on the one hand, for the nurturing of upper-class upper-caste children, and for the survival of her husband on the other. Jashoda is an exemplar of the processes by which mothering is also made a part of waged domestic labour, challenging the universalist assumptions of Western feminists who claim otherwise. Jashoda 'calls into question that aspect of Western Marxist feminism which, from the point of view of work, trivializes the theory of value and, from the point of view of mothering as work, ignores the mother as subject' ('A Literary Representation of the Subaltern' 356). Spivak finds 'native women' doubly oppressed, caught between native patriarchy on the one hand and foreign masculinist-imperialist ideology on the other.

The construction of identity (for both men and women) is influenced by culture, nationality, ethnicity, class and historical differences. The concept of 'woman' as a model which tends to subsume and define all women irrespective of class, race or caste, overrides/obliterates the specificities of the Third World women. Chandra Talpade Mohanty challenges this 'notion of gender or sexual difference, or even patriarchy which can be applied universally and cross-culturally' ('Under Western Eyes' 21). Mohanty critiques the representation of the Third World woman as the 'silent' subject colluding with her othering and voicelessness. She argues that 'native women' are situated at the intersection of multiple discourses and thus possess multiple subjectivities. This challenges the assumptions about 'native women' as the 'silent subaltern'. In 'Under Western Eyes: Feminist Scholarship and Colonial Discourses', Mohanty questions the totalising tendencies of Western feminist discourse: 'The relationship between 'Woman' – a cultural and ideological composite Other constructed through diverse representational discourses (scientific, literary, judicial, linguistic, cinematic, etc) – and 'women' – real, material subjects of their collective histories – is one of the central questions the practice of feminist scholarship seeks to address' (19). Mohanty is sceptical about the monolithic and singular notion of patriarchy revealed by Western feminists, which leads to a reductive notion of a 'third world difference'. The production of this homogenous concept is a way by which Western feminists 'appropriate and "colonize" the constitutive complexities which characterize the lives of women in these countries' (19). This sweeps away the heterogeneity of the lives of Third World women by providing a singular category, complicating the issue of who speaks on behalf of whom. Showing solidarity with the oppressed group cannot be confused with appropriating their voices; the latter is a colonising, patronising/matronising attitude. Mohanty argues in favour of a feminist epistemology that incorporates the differences in the history, location and experiences of Third World women.

In *Feminism Without Borders: Decolonizing Theory, Practicing Solidarity* (2003), Mohanty examines the condition of women in the global capitalist context. The feminist framework she proposes, underlines the racial, economic and political inequalities in a neo-colonial world. She notes that capitalism creates a citizen-consumer nexus that is dependent on the cheap, often-invisible labour of lesser citizens. Herein, the paradigms of heterosexual femininity, domesticity and submissiveness compel Third World women to undertake substandard jobs in the national economy. These subordinated, underpaid, unrecognised workers are denied fundamental rights by the dominant race and sex. Mohanty calls for a transnational female solidarity as a strategy to ensure economic, racial and political stability. In a later essay, '"Under Western Eyes" Revisited', which is a response to the critique of her famous essay 'Under Western Eyes' (1987), Mohanty engages in a personal reflection on her struggles with the definition and the re-definition of her identity vis-à-vis her national and racial affiliations:

> Growing up in India, I was Indian, teaching high school in Nigeria, I was a foreigner.... Doing research in London, I was black. As a professor at an American University, I am an Asian woman . . . in North America I was also a "resident alien" with an Indian passport – I am now a U.S. Citizen whose racialization has shifted dramatically (and negatively) since the attacks on the World Trade Centre and the Pentagon on 11 September 2001. (122)

Rajeswari Sunder Rajan has focused on the image of Indian women in her analysis of the representation of women in colonial and postcolonial contexts. Rajan insists that the ways in which the postcolonial female subjectivity and femininity are inscribed reflect the debates over national identity. The 'native' woman is stereotyped as being without agency, but Rajan contends that it is possible to explore the historically victimised subject position of the 'native' woman as a site 'for the constitution of alternative subjectivities' (10). Rajan and Lata Mani have analysed the debate on the abolition of *sati* to locate female subjectivity in colonial India. The debate on the abolition of *sati* was played out by the colonial discourse, the indigenous conservative discourse and the indigenous liberal discourse. Mani reveals how between these discourses, women were 'neither subjects nor objects, but rather the ground of the discourse on *sati*' (117). The debates and discussions around *sati* were prompted by concerns about Brahmanic scriptures and interpretations of tradition; women were excluded from subject position and deprived of any agency in this discourse. The conservatives lauded *sati* as upholding Hindu tradition. The liberals and the official discourse perceived the woman subjected to *sati* as a victim, either willing or defiant, but essentially moored to Hindu culture. Thus, *sati* as a practice became an 'interlocking ground' of women and tradition:

> Women became emblematic of tradition, and the reworking of tradition is largely conducted through debating the rights and status of women in society. Despite this intimate connection between woman and tradition, or perhaps because of it, these debates are in some sense not primarily about women but about what constitutes authentic cultural tradition. (Mani 90)

Rajan, in her 1993 essay 'The subject of Sati: Pain and Death in the Contemporary Discourse on Sati', discusses the debate on *sati* as a manifestation of a series of binary oppositions subsumed into the larger categories of 'tradition' and 'modernity' (17). Rajan also finds women deprived of their subjectivity or agency in this practice. In an attempt to assign an active subject position to women in *sati*, Rajan calls the practice '*sati*-as-burning' rather than '*sati*-as-death': 'In the case of *sati*, this involves shifting the emphasis from *sati*-as-death (murder or suicide, authentic or inauthentic) to *sati*-as-burning, and investigating both the subjective pain and the objective spectacle that this shift reveals' (19).

Indigenous feminisms existed throughout the colonised world even in the early twentieth century. Leila Ahmed, in her *Women and Gender in Islam: Historical Roots of a Modern Debate* (1992), has documented this phenomenon in the Muslim world. Colonial versions of modernism identified Muslim cultures as an impediment to progress. This negative stereotype was further reinforced using the status of women in Muslim cultures as a litmus test of their cultural advancement/regression. As Ahmed points out, 'The peculiar practices of Islam with respect to women had always formed part of the Western narrative of the quintessential otherness and inferiority of Islam' (149). In *A Quiet Revolution*, Ahmed explores another controversial issue – the use of the *hijab* or the veil. It is an issue which triggers intense debates, regarding the *hijab*'s significance and symbolism. The *hijab* has been perceived as oppressive and discriminatory by the West; it remains a signifier of the 'degradation' of women and the 'backwardness' of a religion to the Western world. This is manifest in the banning of the face-covering veil in France and the partial banning of headscarves for the teachers in Germany. Ahmed herself grew up in a period of Egyptian history (during the reign of Gamal Abdel Nasser, 1956–70) when 'unveiling' was the norm. It was not concomitant with one's religious commitment. On the other hand, during the Iranian revolution in 1979, middle-class women chose to wear the veil as an expression of solidarity with their working-class sisters. Frantz Fanon, in the essay 'Algeria unveiled', from his book *A Dying Colonialism*, reveals the ambiguity of the veil with reference to its use as a camouflage for hiding weapons and supplies by the Algerian women fighting in the anti-colonial resistance. The resurgence of the veil in the Islamic world rekindles the debates surrounding it among Islamists, Muslim feminists, secular Muslims and the Western world. In this context, it is interesting to note the activism and writings of Taslima Nasrin, a Bangladeshi poet and novelist, who came into prominence with her provocative radical feminist views in *Nirbachito Column* (1992), *Lajja* (1993) and her autobiography, *Amar Meyebela* (2002). She incurred the ire of the conservative sections of her community for her uncompromising views and was forced into a life of exile in 1994. Her position as a radical, secular feminist is, however, not above controversy. She has been repeatedly accused of being intentionally inflammatory, of pushing the agenda of international media and political powers. Habiba Zaman, in an article 'The Taslima Nasrin Controversy and Feminism in Bangladesh: A Geopolitical and Transnational Perspective', underlines this paradox: '... the issue was internationally publicized, not to support feminist causes, but to highlight the rise of fundamentalist forces both in Bangladesh and India. Nasrin was a "pawn" in the political game played out by various forces for political gains' (Web, n.p.).

White feminists tend to reduce 'women of colour' or Third World women to just one dimension of their lives (the paradigm of reproduction and housework) and overlook their complex history, variety and subject position. In comparison to coloured/Third World women, white feminists tend to perceive themselves as liberated subjects. Western feminism focuses exclusively on gender discrimination, ignoring other kinds of struggles, such as ethnic struggles, that have gendered dimensions as well. The interests and experiences of women from marginalised groups challenge this exclusionary approach of Western feminism.

Trinh T. Minh-ha, a Vietnamese writer, composer and filmmaker, reviews the categories of women, in her *Woman, Native, Other: Writing Postcoloniality and Feminism* (1989). Minh-ha critiques the relationship between the First World feminists and their marginal counterparts in Third World. She questions the homogenising tendencies of First World feminism that tend to undermine the diversity of the Third World woman. She suggests that First World feminists have excluded the concerns of Third World women just as men have traditionally excluded and subordinated women. This politics of oppression is common to both racism and sexism. Minh-ha suggests that linearity of thought and language reinforces authority; she criticises objectivity in writing as being alienating, especially for women. Minh-ha admits that the use of language is inevitable, but as a writer and filmmaker, she prefers to privilege the body rather than the mind. She incorporates several female voices in her book – Toni Morrison, Audre Lorde, Nellie Wong, Gloria Anzaldua, Leslie Marmon Silko – to represent the heterogeneity and multiplicity inscribed within the category of the 'other'. The binary polarity of self-other, by which the Third World woman is understood vis-à-vis the First World white woman, is inadequate to decipher the differences and diversity in the category of the 'Third World woman'. In an interview with Pratibha Parmar, Minh-ha insists, '. . . a critical space of differentiation needs to be maintained since issues specifically raised by Third World women have less to do with questions of cultural difference than with a different notion of feminism itself – how it is lived and how it is practiced' (Parmar 151).

In India, feminism has been a problematic concept since it is either viewed as alienating from indigenous culture and tradition or as non-cognisant of class issues. In both these cases, the underlying belief is that feminism is a Western ideology, synonymous with the unrestricted freedom enjoyed by women unbound by traditions and responsibilities. Historically, the 'woman question' was debated alongside the nationalist struggle in the nineteenth century; for the colonisers, the inferiority of the colonised culture was gauged by women's status in Indian society. The existence of the practices of *sati*, female infanticide, child marriage and *purdah*, and the lack of female education reinforced the cultural stereotype of the natives as barbaric, primitive and uncivilised. It is, however, noteworthy that native reform groups such as the Brahmo Samaj, the Arya Samaj and the National Social Conference worked actively towards 'modernising' and 'Westernising' women. This was necessitated by the inculcation of Western education by the native elite. Reformers such as Raja Ram Mohan Roy (1772–1833) and Ishwar Chandra Vidyasagar (1820–91) worked towards the progressive ideals of widow remarriage and women's education and the abolition of regressive practices such as *sati* and polygamy. Jyotiba Phule (1827–90), Savitribai Phule (1831–97) and Pandita Ramabai (1858–1922) were radical and iconoclastic in their personal lives and political attitudes. Jyotiba Phule's analysis of the gender-caste discriminatory axis anticipates the central debate of Dalit feminism.

The emancipation of women in nineteenth- and early-twentieth-century India has been seen in terms of the conflicting agendas of the 'revivalists' (tending towards tradition and conventions vis-à-vis women's role and function in society and family) and the 'modernists' (inclined towards the models inculcated by Western education). Partha Chatterjee, in 'The Nationalist Resolution of the Woman's Question', refers to this home-world dichotomy: 'In the main, this resolution was built around a separation of the domain of culture into two spheres – the material and the spiritual' (239). According to Chatterjee's analysis, women were assigned responsibility of retaining and sustaining the spiritual essence of the national life along with acquiring literacy and techniques of modern housekeeping, while men were expected to learn the ways of the 'world', the superior intellectual ability to fight the imperial domination. Chatterjee is, however, quick to point out, 'The new patriarchy which nationalist discourse set up as a hegemonic construct . . . has generalized itself among the new middle class . . . but is irrelevant to the large mass of subordinate classes' (251). The participation of women in the nationalist movement and their entry into the public sphere question this home-world binary. In 1901, Sarala Devi Chaudhurani (1872–1945) formed the Bharat Stri Mahamandal, following differences with the male leadership of the National Social Conference. In 1917, Sarojini Naidu (1879–1949) led a delegation of women to the Constitutional Reforms Committee, demanding universal adult franchise. It was not just an elitist 'participation from above', but nationalist revolutionaries such as Bina Das (1911–86), Pritilata Waddedar (1911–32), Kalpana Datta (1913–95) and Matangini Hazra (1870–1942) suggest a wider participation. While there are instances of sensationalisation and misrepresentation of Indian practices, as reflected in Katherine Mayo's *Mother India* (1927), there are examples of Annie Besant (1847–1933) and Margaret Cousins (1878–1954) who were staunch critics of imperialism and chose to adopt India as their home. The All India Women's Conference and the National Federation of Indian Women emerged, and under the leadership of Mahatma Gandhi, actively participated in the nationalist anti-colonial struggle.

Since Independence, Indian feminism has become more amorphous, engaging with issues such as female foeticide, dowry-deaths, sexual violence, equality in the workplace and sexual freedom. A government-commissioned report in 1974 indicated that women's condition in India has declined since Independence. This report, which was named 'Toward Equality', provided a necessary impetus to the feminist movement, which was further fermented by other social and political incidents. Peasants' movement, working-class movements and ecological activism such as the 'Chipko' movement found women in positions of leadership. The declaration of the Emergency in 1975 interrupted the women's movement in India temporarily; but by 1977, certain significant changes emerged. Women's groups were formed all over the major cities of India, usually with Leftist leanings, composed of the urban intelligentsia. However, these autonomous women's groups, generally working in tandem with organised political parties, often remained cut off from the common mass of Indian women. Ilina Sen points out this ambivalence: 'the women's platforms emerging in the context of mass movements do not necessarily provide women with significant representation in the leadership of the overall movements' (qtd. in Chaudhuri 201). The 1980s and 90s witnessed attacks on feminist movements from conservative quarters. The Shah Bano case (1985) and the Roop Kanwar Sati case (1987) raised several questions about equal rights for women irrespective of religion, caste and class.

The role of the family and community is especially pertinent to the issue of feminism in India, the conflict between 'confrontation' and 'compromise' taking centre stage. Madhu Kishwar, a feminist activist and founder of *Manushi*, underscores this anomaly: 'In India, most of us find it difficult to tune in to the extreme individualism that comes to us through feminism. For instance, most women here are unwilling to assert their rights in a way that estranges them not just from their family, but also from their larger kinship group and community' (272).

Dalit feminism insists on reviewing the categories of caste and gender not as mutually exclusive and discrete, but rather as connected and influencing each other. There are, however, contentions regarding the matter of understanding, and the representation of, the specific marginalisation and dispossession suffered by Dalit women by 'Indian' feminists, who are accused of adopting a universalist and totalising attitude towards the issue. Dalit feminism challenges the unisonant voice of Indian feminism and rejects any attempts of representation of their cause as inauthentic. In their view, Indian feminism (or what goes by the name) fails to address and acknowledge caste-based oppression of women. Kum-kum Bhavnani and Meg Coulson, while discussing the issue of race in feminist theory, point out a similar kind of discrepancy, 'While inequalities between states have increased, inequalities and differences between and within classes and peoples have also increased, including inequalities amongst women' (76). Like black women, Dalit women challenge the complacency of feminists in their project of seeing 'woman' as a homogenous category without differences in their historicity, class, caste, race and sexuality. Dalit women share a similar attitude towards Indian feminism which they find to be ideologically 'savarna' and belonging to the upper middle class. Gopal Guru terms Dalit feminism as a 'politics of difference' (80) since it is directed against dual patriarchal structures that tend to oppress Dalit women – the brahminical patriarchy that discriminates against them on the basis of caste and the patriarchal exploitation perpetrated by Dalit men, which operates on more insidious and intimate levels. The formation of the National Federation for Dalit Women (NFDW) presents a significant moment in the history of the feminist movement in India that challenges and subverts the tendency of Indian feminism to speak for Indian women as a homogeneous entity.

Dalit feminists have defined the three-way oppression suffered by Dalit women: (1) as the subject of caste oppression at the hands of the upper castes; (2) as labourers subject to class-based oppression, also mainly at the hands of the upper and middle castes; and (3) as women who experience patriarchal oppression at the hands of all men, including the men of their own caste. The NGO Declaration on Gender and Racism, adopted by the NFDW in the World Conference Against Racism, held in Durban in 2001, is crucial in understanding the real nature of their oppression, their vulnerabilities and fears: 'We recognize that the relationship between gender and distinct forms of racism, therefore in the Asian and particularly Indian context, typifies the particularity of the condition of women belonging to the Dalits. . .' (qtd. in Rao 365). Dalit feminism therefore marks a shift from the preoccupation with 'woman', as a category, to an awareness and inclusion of 'women' in the scope of feminist theory, underscoring the importance of acknowledging 'feminisms' instead of 'feminism'.

Dalit feminism tackles the issue of identity politics in widening the scope of feminism to include several differences in approach and attitude. Dalit women's writing forms a significant part of this project of destabilising predominant discourse(s). Dalit women writers challenge and subvert several positions including those adopted by the 'savarna' patriarchy and the Dalit patriarchy. What is interesting, however, is that Dalit women's writings (taking a lead from the theoretical basis of Dalit feminism) refuse to be represented by women writers who are insensitive to the interface between caste and gender in their writings. It is aimed at an exploration of these axes between caste and gender that cause the intensification of their oppression. In this respect, Meenakshi Moon and Urmila Pawar's *We also Made History* is path-breaking. The aim of the work is to record the contribution made by Dalit women to the Phule-Ambedkarite movement. The project is daunting since it is a historical reconstruction of an oppressed and unarticulated past of a section of people who have been traditionally and historically relegated to the background. It needs to be understood that such non-fictional work, which is not based on an imaginative resurrection of an exploited existence, but is a result of grass-root-level research and documentation, represents a certain kind of intellectual activism. Dalit women's writing is not just the expression of aesthetic pleasure but is permeated with the awareness of a discriminatory society. Sharmila Rege points out, in her *Writing Caste/Writing Gender*, 'Dalit women's testimonies offered counter narratives that challenged the selective memory and univocal history both of the Dalit and the women's movement' (75). Thus the articulation of the trauma and anger by Dalit women in their writing has a definite political dimension.

'US Third World feminism' addresses the intersection of race, ethnicity and gender. Chela Sandoval, an important theorist of US Third World feminism, locates the origin of the movement between the years 1968 and 1990. This approach challenges the exclusionary politics of the First World structure of gender, class, race and sexuality, and moves between 'equal rights', 'revolutionary', 'supremacist' and 'separatist' ideologies, to arrive at the fifth possibility of subverting the hegemonic order, which she names the 'differential consciousness'. This approach incorporates different strategies and attitudes to transcend the hegemonic mode of mainstream feminism. It is not aimed at carving out a 'singular' identity but advocates a strategy, which emerges from the life experiences and the realities of poverty and exclusion, which cannot be addressed by any one ideology. This provides marginalised groups with the flexibility to manoeuvre their tactics according to the nature of the oppression they confront. In the *Methodology of Oppression*, Sandoval poses serious challenges to feminism and women's studies. She identifies the politics of erasure that is aimed at US Third World feminism and undertakes to flout it. She outlines a four-phase feminist history of consciousness – 'Liberal', 'Marxist', 'Radical' and 'Socialist'. Despite their differences, there is a common link between these four in their indifference and non-inclusion of US Third World feminism. Sandoval argues that the evolving mainstream feminist discourse failed to incorporate the concerns of marginalised gender groups in the US, such as African,

Asian and South American women. These groups have been added to feminist theory only at the level of description, but they have hardly ever been acknowledged as contributing to the theory *per se*. By providing a five-fold structure of alternative, and oppositional ideology, Sandoval proposes to explode the hegemonic feminist ideology. *This Bridge Called My Back: Writings by Radical Women of Color* (1981), edited by Gloria Anzaldúa and Cherríe Moraga, falls under the rubric of US Third World feminism. Other significant works by women of colour are *Making Waves: An Anthology of Writings by and about Asian American Women* (1989) edited by the Asian Women United in California, and Audre Lorde's *Sister Outsider* (1984). US Third World feminism has emerged as an important movement within postcolonial feminism that aspires to be multiple, polylithic and culture-specific.

SHORT TAKES

STRATEGIC ESSENTIALISM

Strategic essentialism is a way by which women struggle against sexism but at the same time perform the 'feminine' to survive and meet their goals. It is predicated on the understanding that essentialism is unavoidable and needs to be critiqued but it can also be used to mediate the complexities of the social and political world. Gayatri Chakravorty Spivak provided postcolonial and feminist theory with the concept of 'strategic essentialism' as a way of resistance, though it implied a temporary closure of meaning in the stereotype. For marginalised and minority groups, deploying strategic essentialism or accepting an essentialist identity, can have short-term effectiveness, unless, of course, this is cast as a more permanent stereotype. It is a context-specific tactic and cannot be a long-term action against oppression. It can be practised in day-to-day life or can be used as a tool in political action. Spivak rejects essentialism on the grounds that it implies the stable meaning of a particular category, but espouses the use of essentialism as a 'strategy', but never as a 'theory'. For example, appealing to ethnic/sexual/racial identity can ensure ways of negotiating and combating discrimination but it can only be situational.

CHICANO FEMINISM

It is a political movement generated by the working-class women of Mexican descent living in the United States. They identify racism, sexism and classism as factors deployed against them. The term 'Chicano' refers to the people of Mexican descent living in the US and is derived from a common oral usage in working-class communities. The Chicano movements of the 1960s intersected with other movements such as Black Power, the Anti-Vietnam War movement and the Civil Rights. Chicano feminists, however, were dissatisfied with their representation in the movement, and eventually formed distinct, separate identities to challenge Anglo and Chicano patriarchies and Anglo feminism as well. Chicano feminism inaugurated the exploration of the Chicano literary tradition that had remained unvoiced. Chicano feminism adds to feminist theory by centring the race-class-gender-sexuality nexus in their analyses.

THE SUBALTERN

The term 'subaltern' literally means 'a junior officer in the British army'. The term came into theoretical discourse with Antonio Gramsci, who, in his *Prison Notebooks*, used the term to denote subordinate groups or classes. In particular, 'subaltern' in Gramscian theory referred to the peasants of Southern Italy who had no social or political solidarity as a group, and therefore were dominated by the hegemonic discourse of power. The word has an extended association with a group of historians, the Subaltern Collective, to signify the subordinate groups of South Asia, who were marginalised based on caste, class, age, gender and office. Gayatri Chakravorty Spivak drew upon deconstructionism, Marxism and feminism to interrogate the location of the subaltern in her celebrated essay, 'Can the Subaltern Speak?' The answer is 'no', since, she argues, the heterogeneity of the subaltern cannot find a unitary voice. Moreover, the subaltern is denied subject position in the Indian and English discourses to either know or represent itself. The subalternity of the woman, especially in the colonial context, is more acute, since she has neither the conceptual language nor the audience of the colonial or the native

> men who would hear her. It is not that subaltern women cannot speak, but they have been denied the subject position in the colonial discourse and are therefore condemned to silence.

REFERENCES

Ahmed, Leila. *Women and Gender in Islam: Historical Roots of a Modern Debate*. Michigan: Yale UP, 1992. Print.

Bhavnani, Kum-kum and Meg Coulson. 'Race.' *A Concise Companion to Feminist Theory*. Ed. Mary Eagleton. Oxford: Blackwell, 2003. 73–92. Print.

Chatterjee, Partha. 'The Nationalist Resolution of the Women's Question.' *Recasting Women: Essays in Colonial History*. Ed. Kumkum Sangari and Suresh Vaid. New Delhi: Kali for Women, 1989. 233–53. Print.

Chaudhuri, Maitrayee. *Feminism in India*. New Delhi: Kali for Women, 2004. Print.

Guru, Gopal. 'Dalit Women Talk Differently.' *Gender and Caste*. Ed. Anupama Rao. New Delhi: Kali for Women, 2005. 80–85. Print.

Kishwar, Madhu. *Off the Beaten Track: Rethinking Gender Justice for Indian Women*. New Delhi: Oxford UP, 1999. Print.

Mani, Lata. 'Contentious Traditions: The Debate on Sati in Colonial India.' *Recasting Women: Essays in Colonial History*. Ed. Kumkum Sangari and Suresh Vaid. New Delhi: Kali for Women, 1989. 88–126. Print.

Mills, Sara. 'Postcolonial Feminist Theory.' *Contemporary Feminist Theories*. Ed. Stevi Jackson. Edinburgh: Edinburgh UP, 1998. 98–112. Print.

Mohanty, Chandra Talpade. 'Under Western Eyes: Feminist Scholarship and Colonial Discourses.' *Feminism without Borders: Decolonizing Theory, Practising Solidarity*. Durham and London: Duke UP, 2003. 17–42. Print.

---. '"Under Western Eyes" Revisited: Feminist Solidarity through Anticapitalist Struggles.' *Feminism without Borders: Decolonizing Theory, Practising Solidarity*. Durham and London: Duke UP, 2003. 221–51. Print.

Parmar, Pratibha. 'Between Theory and Poetry.' *Framer Framed*. Ed. Trinh T. Min-ha. New York: Routledge, 1992. 151–59. Print.

Rajan, Rajeswari Sunder. 'The Subject of Sati: Pain and Death in the Contemporary Discourse on Sati.' *Real and Imagined Women: Gender, Culture and Postcolonialism*. New York: Routledge, 2003. 15–38. Print.

Rao, Anupama, ed. *Gender and Caste*. New Delhi: Kali for Women, 2005. Print.

Rege, Sharmila. *Writing Caste/Writing Gender: Narrating Dalit Women's Testimonies*. New Delhi: Zubaan, 2006. Print.

Sandoval, Chela. *Methodology of the Oppressed*. Minneapolis: Minnesota Press, 2000. Print.

Spivak, Gayatri Chakravorty. 'Feminism and Critical Theory.' *In Other Worlds: Essays in Cultural Politics*. New York: Routledge, 1988. 102–24. Print.

---. 'French Feminism in an International Frame.' *In Other Worlds: Essays in Cultural Politics*. New York: Routledge, 1988. 184–211. Print.

---. 'A Literary Representation of the Subaltern.' *In Other Worlds: Essays in Cultural Politics*. New York: Routledge, 2006. 332–70. Print.

Zaman, Habiba. 'The Taslima Nasrin Controversy and Feminism in Bangladesh: A Geo-Political and Transnational Representation.' *Atlantis* 23.2 (Spring/Summer1999). Web. 18 November 2013. <journals.msvu.ca/index.php/atlantis/article/download/1651/1411>.

Chapter Nine
Ecofeminism

Ecofeminism as a theory developed in the 1970s, alongside environmental and other radical political movements, especially with the publication of Rachel Carson's (1907–64) *The Silent Spring* (1962). The term 'ecofeminism' first appeared in the year 1974, in Françoise d'Eaubonne's (1920–2005) *Le féminisme ou la mort*. According to the tenets of ecofeminism, women have an affirmative and close relationship with nature. This is due to the female reproductive role and mothering nature, which brings them closer to the rhythm of nature. However, the role of women as nurturers renders them more vulnerable to the consequences of ecological destruction. Ecofeminists believe that there exists a direct link between the oppression of nature and the oppression of women; sexism and naturism are inseparable. To understand the nature of women's oppression one needs to understand the oppression of nature. Since patriarchy is based on dualism – privileging the mind over the body, the male over the female, culture over nature – it creates and discriminates against the 'other' of the dyad. Ecofeminism seeks to address this imbalance by connecting nature with women. Ecofeminism insists that feminist theory needs to include the ecological perspective, and solutions to ecological problems must address the feminist perspective.

Mary Mellor in *Feminism and Ecology* defines ecofeminism thus:

> Eco-feminism brings together elements of the feminist and the green movement, while at the same time offering a challenge to both. It takes from the green movement the concern about the impact of human activities on the non-human world and

from feminism the view of humanity as gendered in ways that subordinate, exploit and oppress women. (1)

Ecofeminism as a theory developed alongside other political and resistance movements. It has also incorporated concerns about race and class. Though not uniform, ecofeminism has its provenance in ecology (biological, spiritual, social) and feminism (Liberal, Radical, Socialist, Marxist). As Val Plumwood points out,

> From early and Liberal feminism, it (ecofeminism) takes the impulse to integrate women fully as part of human culture and from socialist feminism, it draws an understanding of the processes and structures of power and domination. From radical feminism, it takes the critiques of the masculinity of dominant culture and the aspiration to replace it, to affirm what has been denigrated. (qtd. in Mack-Canty 169)

'Deep ecologists', like ecofeminists, believe in the inseparability of nature and people. They believe that nature has an intrinsic value and needs to be preserved even if it necessitates the curtailment of the human use of nature. However, according to a section of ecofeminists, deep ecologists overlook a vital issue of environmental degradation – the problem is not anthropocentrism as identified by deep ecologists, but androcentrism. Ecofeminists argue that the problem lies with the male-centredness of Western culture that causes both sexism and naturism. Luc Ferry, in *New Ecological Order*, summarises the views of Ariel Salleh, the Australian social ecologist and ecofeminist, and other like-minded ecofeminists in the following manner: 'the hatred of women, which ipso facto brings about that of nature, is one of the principal mechanisms governing the actions of men (of 'male') and, thus, the whole of Western/patriarchal culture' (118).

Maria Mies, a sociologist and an eminent theorist of ecofeminism, points out that since women are more involved than men in daily life, they are more engaged with the elements of nature. Both Mies and Vandana Shiva, another influential ecofeminist, condemn the capitalist and patriarchal tendency of eliding differences and imposing sameness. They also expose the consequences of an alienating capitalist culture. In an essay titled 'White Man's

Dilemma: His Search for What He has Destroyed', Mies makes a strong case against the capitalist patriarchal tendency of exoticising nature as a getaway or wilderness, which they have mindlessly destroyed in their materialist and profit-driven enterprises. In this context, she refers to the tourist publicity material of First World countries where they sell the 'native' experiences in close proximity with nature in Third World countries. This phenomenon, she insists, is illustrative of treating nature as a colony or dominion for exploitation and subjugation. A similar kind of master-slave form is operative in men's behaviour towards women. In the capitalist patriarchal model, the male tendency of treating nature as a commodity to be used and harnessed is extended to their intention of treating women's bodies as a sexual commodity. Shiva and Mies give instances of the resistance offered by women protesting against ecological devastation that endangers their existence. Shiva refers to the Chipko movement of 1974 where several women of the Indian Himalayan region started an unusual protest movement to prevent the felling of indigenous trees. They physically hugged the trees to save them ('chipko' means 'to hug' in Hindi), since they considered these trees integral to the subsistence economy, as a resistance against the project of replacing them by planting commercially lucrative eucalyptus trees. This movement was significant on several levels. As Shiva points out, the Chipko movement was a female-dominated environmental movement to save trees as well as a politico-social movement against the Western model of development.

The works of Shiva and Mies represent the subsistence model against a consumerist, profit-driven, technical lifestyle. The subsistence model emphasises the synthesis/synergy between technological advancement and traditional wisdom. Natural resources, according to this formulation, should not be treated as 'possessions' and exploited beyond human need. Men and women need to develop a lifestyle which is attuned to nature, more communitarian than isolated. This subsistence model is often accused of being limited in its effectiveness but it surely provides the possibility of a radical alternative to the Western forms of modern, industrial, capitalist ways of thinking. It underscores the relevance and the value of traditional wisdom and economic models.

Other movements that provided the impetus to ecofeminism include: Lois Gibbs's efforts to expose the fact that Love Canal in Niagra Falls, New York state, was a toxic waste site (1979); the Green Belt Movement (1977) in Kenya initiated by Wangari Maathai where rural women planted trees to prevent deforestation and desertification of land; and the Greening of Harlem Coalition (1989) by Bernadette Cozart to restore the rundown Harlem into green spaces. Ecofeminism thus also addresses issues such as deforestation, toxic waste, nuclear weapon policies, agricultural policies, development, technology and animal rights.

Ecofeminism, in its use of an interdependence model of nature and human beings, is inspired by Carol Gilligan's 'ethics of care', which insists on the necessity of taking into consideration the needs of not only the human but also the non-human world. Ecofeminism tries to bring together local activism and a global perspective. There are several strands to the philosophy of ecofeminism. One strand insists on the importance of the well-being of the earth; another strand emphasises the sacredness of the earth; and a third strand underscores the importance of sustainability in using the earth's resources.

Ecofeminist literary criticism as a genre has emerged to evaluate literature from feminist and ecological perspectives. Ecofeminist theologians such as Starhawk (Miriam Simos), Charlene Spretnak and Carol Christ emphasise the spiritual aspect of the interconnectedness between women and nature. The 'spiritual ecofeminists' use the concept of the 'Goddess' to challenge the androcentrism of the Judeo-Christian and Western myths, rituals and spiritual practices. As Stephen Lahar points out, 'Ecofeminist political goals include the deconstruction of oppressive social, economic and political systems and the reconstruction of more viable social and political forms' (qtd. in Warren 35–36).

> **SHORT TAKES**
>
> **DEEP ECOLOGY**
>
> Norwegian philosopher and mountaineer Arne Dekke Eide Næss (1912–2009) introduced the concept of 'deep ecology'. He provided the framework of two kinds of environmentalism – the 'long range deep ecology movement' and the 'shallow ecology movement'. Deep ecology questions the root or fundamental causes of the degradation of ecology, while the shallow ecology movement promotes immediate remedies such as recycling to address the issue of environmental degradation caused by the industrial abuse of natural resources. Deep ecology philosophy asserts the importance and the intrinsic value of all beings and things and the need to save them from the agents of destruction. Deep ecology emphasises ecological wisdom, preservation of biodiversity and indigenous practices.

REFERENCES

Ferry, Luc. *The New Ecological Order*. Chicago: The U of Chicago P, 1995. Print.

Mack-Canty, Colleen. 'Third Wave Feminism and the Need to Reweave Nature/Culture Duality.' *NWSA Journal* 6.3 (Autumn 2004). 154–79. Web. 12 March 2015. <http:www.jstor.org/stable/43107085>.

Mies, Maria. 'White Man's Dilemma: His Search for What He has Destroyed.' *Ecofeminism: Critique, Influence, Change*. Ed. Maria Mies and Vandana Shiva. London: Zed Books, 1993. 132–62. Print.

Mellor, Mary. *Feminism and Ecology*. New York: New York UP, 1997. Print.

Shiva, Vandana. 'The *Chipko* Women's Concept of Freedom.' *Ecofeminism: Critique, Influence, Change*. Ed. Maria Mies and Vandana Shiva. London: Zed Books, 1993. 246–49. Print.

Warren, Karen. *Ecofeminist Philosophy: A Western Perspective on What It Is and Why It Matters*. London: Rowman and Littlefield, 2000. Print.

Chapter Ten
Lesbian Feminism

Lesbian feminism offered a separatist and positive vision of community in feminist ideology. It offered a model of women's counter-culture, not only as a strategy of achieving women's liberation but as the meaning and purpose of feminism. The tropes of identity, sexuality and community are integral to lesbian feminism. As Caroline Gonda points out,

> Separately or in conjunction, those concerns prompt a whole range of Lesbian theoretical writings: from the 1960s to the 1990s; from grass-roots pamphlets to high-academic monographs; and across disciplines from anthropology, ethics, history, philosophy, politics, psychology or sociology to literary criticism, film studies, cultural studies, rhetoric or pure theory. (113)

Lesbian feminism emerged from the dissatisfaction with 'second-wave feminism'; it challenged heteronormativity as a socio-cultural institution and argued that lesbianism is the only form of emancipated sexuality since it excludes men, and subsequently, rejects patriarchy.

In 1972, Adrienne Rich (1929–2012) argued for a radical reinterpretation of old texts to unearth the alternative female voice subverting the heterosexist literary culture. Rich believed that women occupied a 'lesbian continuum' that might not always involve sexual relationships. In 'Compulsory Heterosexuality and Lesbian Existence', Rich contends that heterosexuality is imposed forcibly upon women by patriarchy to control the female mind and body. Lesbianism, she insists, is not just a sexual practice but a possibility of a female identity beyond patriarchy.

Bonnie Zimmerman raises some pertinent questions related to the role of the lesbians in constructing, receiving and interpreting literature. The essential question that Zimmerman raises is whether lesbianism offers a separate aesthetic vantage. She asserts that lesbian feminist criticism disestablishes heterosexual norms and also provides a unique lesbian perspective of a separate identity predicated upon a 'woman-identification' or love between women.

Barbara Smith, in 'Towards a Black Feminist Criticism' (1977), problematises the representation of women by white feminists and black male critics; she accuses them of ignoring black women's literature and excluding black lesbian creativity altogether. Monique Wittig, the French author and literary theorist, goes a step further in dismantling the sexual divide in society by questioning the category of sex in her work, which itself challenges the boundary between fiction and theory. Teresa de Lauretis, in 'Sexual Indifference and Lesbian Representation' (1988), presents a survey of varied cultural productions and concludes that gender binaries are necessary for reinforcing the tyranny of patriarchy. The transformation of the stereotypes of sex, gender and sexuality can be achieved only through analysing lesbian identities as heterogeneous, significant and continuously trying to escape fixed definitions.

Lesbian feminists consider themselves doubly oppressed. As women they already occupy a marginal status in society; they are doubly marginalised in their minority location as lesbians. Martha Shelley, in 'Notes of a Radical Lesbian', recounts the hostility that lesbian women receive from heterosexual men and women. Men fear lesbianism as a threat to their supremacy, while straight women resent lesbians because they represent an alternative which, according to them, is separatist.

The position of lesbians in the feminist movement has been a contentious issue. They were accused of being a 'lavendar menace', by Betty Friedan, irritants as well as vanguards, for their complete refusal to be defined in relation to men. Lesbian feminists claim lesbianism to be the quintessential feminism. They consider social constructions around gender binaries causative of women's oppression. Men assume the dominant role imposing submissive, diffident roles on women, in order to perpetuate hetero-patriarchy. Lesbian feminism, in the trope of 'woman-identified woman', absolutely negates the male presence by locating sexual and emotional desire only among women. The sex-gender dichotomy is reinvented in lesbianism. Since sex is biological and gender is socially constructed, the categories of masculinity and femininity are re-mediated in the lesbian context. Judith Butler points out,

> When the constructed status of gender is theorized as radically independent of sex, gender itself becomes a free-floating artifice, with the consequence that man and masculine might just as easily signify a female body as a male one, and a woman and feminine a male body as easily as a female one. (6)

The 'Radicalesbians' group published a manifesto in 1970, 'The Woman-Identified Woman'. The manifesto launched a severe attack against the stereotypes imposed on women and called for the sexual liberty of women from heterosexual norms:

> Only women can give to each other a new sense of self. That identity we have to develop with reference to ourselves, and not in relation to men. This consciousness is the revolutionary force from which all else will follow, for ours is an organic revolution. For this we must be available and supportive to one another, give our commitment and our love, give the emotional support necessary to sustain this movement. Our energies must flow towards our sisters not backwards towards our oppressor. (qtd. in Blasius and Phelan 399)

Lesbian feminism is typified by the assertion of difference and a desire to break the mould of the established order of things. It challenges the celebration of reproductive motherhood and the virtues of passive femininity valorised by the patriarchal paradigm. Lesbian feminism privileges multiplicity of meaning, resisting normative classifications and expressing scepticism about the underlying pattern of domination persistent in male logocentrism. It identifies heteronormativity as causative of the retention of male supremacy in a deeply fractious society. The trajectory of lesbian feminism reveals a bias towards a separatist politics, and an anxiety over the claim of heterosexual women on the feminist movement, since they were considered more as the collaborators of patriarchy. Lesbian feminism is predicated on the need for lesbians to situate themselves historically, establish a sense of community and to ascribe a positive sense of identity to this community.

> **SHORT TAKES**
>
> ### QUEER THEORY
>
> Queer theory suggests a body of work that explores gay, lesbian and bisexual life experiences. It seeks to define/redefine the ways in which sexual identities are constituted in contemporary culture. The term 'queer' is provocative and challenges normative lifestyles and attitudes. Judith Butler insists that gender is performative and destabilises the hegemonic, heterosexual assumptions constructing subjectivity. Michel Foucault's *The History of Sexuality Vol I* is generally credited with inaugurating mainstream queer theory in academia. Butler and Eve Sedgewick have combined gay and lesbian politics, feminist insights and postmodern conditions to produce fraught accounts of sexuality and gender that subvert essentialist notions of these categories. The agenda of queer theory is to fill in the gaps and silences of the hetero-centric discourse and eradicate bigotry and prejudice. Feminist and queer theories have a complicated intersectionality. Both interrogate the ideological structures of sex, gender and sexuality; but queer theory's 'positive' emphasis on sexuality is not always shared by feminist theory.

> **SHORT TAKES**
>
> ### RADICALLESBIANS
>
> This was a group that emerged in the 1970s as a challenge to the contemporary mainstream feminist movement's exclusionary politics that treated the lesbian presence in the feminist movement as a 'lavender menace'. The group was spearheaded by Rita Mae Brown and they formulated the first major lesbian manifesto 'The Woman-Identified-Woman'. The manifesto exposed the inadequacies of the 70s' feminist movement in accommodating the concerns and voices of the lesbians. Radical lesbians as a group inaugurated the shift from second-wave feminism to the more diverse engagements of third-wave feminism.

REFERENCES

Blasius, Mark, and Shane Phelan, ed. *We are Everywhere: A Historical Sourcebook of Gay and Lesbian Politics.* New York: Routledge, 1997. Print.

Butler, Judith. *Gender Trouble: Feminism and the Subversion of Identity.* New York: Routledge, 1990. Print.

Gonda, Caroline. 'Lesbian Theory.' *Contemporary Feminist Theories.* Ed. Stevi Jackson and Jackie Jones. Edinburgh: Edinburgh UP, 1998. 113–30. Print.

Chapter Eleven

Feminist Criticism in Practice

Myths, legends and fairy tales are often repositories of gender stereotypes with underlying possibilities of subversion. The three texts used here for analysis have been chosen deliberately to bring out this fact. The first section of this chapter discusses the enigma of Draupadi in history and myth from a feminist perspective, based on Iravati Karve's *Yuganta* and Saoli Mitra's *Five Lords, Yet None a Protector* (translation of *Nathabati Anathabat*). The second section analyses the feminist retelling of Perrault's 'Red Riding Hood' by Angela Carter in the short story, 'The Company of Wolves' from the anthology *Bloody Chamber and Other Stories*.

1

Iravati Karve (1905–70) was a renowned anthropologist, educationist, pioneering researcher and feminist scholar. *Yuganta: The End of an Epoch*, her study of the characters and society in the *Mahabharata*, was first published in Marathi in 1967 and later translated into English in 1969. *Yuganta* explores the major mythical-heroic figures of the *Mahabharata* from historical and anthropological perspectives. Karve takes on the role of a critical interventionist and examines the acclaimed characters rationally, revealing in the process, the relevance of the epic in contemporary times. In this collection of essays, she discusses the major characters, contexts and settings in order to look at the old text from a fresh perspective. In the essay on Draupadi, Karve initiates a comparative discourse that focuses on Sita (the major female protagonist in the epic *Ramayana*) and Draupadi, assigning a greater complexity to the latter. She tries to re-imagine Draupadi's life vis-à-vis the tradition and history of the contemporary society.

Yuganta is the earliest instance of a feminist revisionary analysis of the epic. Karve attempts to demystify the magical-divine complex that lies at the centre of Draupadi's *swayamvara* and Arjun's heroic feat at winning Draupadi's hand:

> Till the date they married Draupadi, the Pandavas travelled incognito from town to town. They had escaped the horrible death planned for them by Kauravas, and were afraid of letting their enemies know that they are alive. In the court of Drupada they sat, under assumed identities, among a group of poor Brahmins. Arjuna's success in the contest won for the Pandavas not only a beautiful wife but also powerful allies. With these allies and the Yadavas to back them, they could ask for their share of the Hastinapur kingdom. Through their marriage to Draupadi, they got a wife, status and a kingdom. (77)

While focusing upon Draupadi's tumultuous life, Karve humanises this epic figure and assigns the responsibility for her sufferings to the patriarchal framework of society. In the concluding section of the essay, Karve imaginatively reconstructs Draupadi's last hours, when she sets out with her husbands on their last pilgrimage. Karve imbues it with her commentary and departs from the original text, where the fatigued Draupadi and the Pandavas, except for Yudhisthir and his dog, fall down. Draupadi is presented in a moment of crisis when she gains an insight into the real nature of her husbands; she comprehends Yudhisthir's contempt conveyed in his scathing comment: 'She fell because she loved Arjuna the most' (92). Perhaps, for the first time, Draupadi realises the magnitude of Yudhisthir's feelings of inadequacy, compared to Arjun. She also reviews the undercurrents of her relationship with Arjun. She is guilty as charged by Yudhisthir; she had perhaps loved Arjun above all else but perhaps it had not been the same for Arjun – as the long line of women in Arjun's life (Ulupi, Chitrangada, Subhadra) proves. In Karve's reconstruction, Draupadi is pierced by the sudden realisation that it was Bhima who had always railed against the world for her. The essay ends on a poignant note with Draupadi pleading with Bhima in her last moments: 'In our next birth be the eldest, Bhima: under your shelter we all can live in safety and joy' (95).

If Karve's is the earliest feminist retelling of the Draupadi myth, Saoli Mitra's *Five Lords, Yet None a Protector* extends the strategy of subverting the grand narrative, manifesting, in the process, Kristeva's assertion that, 'Any text is constructed as a mosaic of quotations, any text is the absorption and transformation of another' (66). Michael and Judith Still argue that 'the two axes of intertextuality, texts entering via authors (who are first readers), and text entering via readers, the co-producers of meaning' are both emotionally and politically charged (qtd. in Wardle 103). Mitra's *Nathabati Anathabat* is operative on both these axes. The 'new' text articulates the unarticulated, illuminates the hidden, and debunks the preconceived paradigms of the normative of the 'old' text, and at the same time, reveals the 'influence' of another 'intertext'.

Karve's *Yuganta* is a perceivable influence in Mitra's play, but the latter introduces other elements, which add depth and range to the new interpretation of the old text. In this transformation from an epic to a drama, Mitra employs an indigenous tradition of storytelling, the *'kathakathan'*. The role of the *'kathak-thakur'* or storyteller is appropriated by a female voice; Mitra uses a *'kathak-thakuran'* in place of a male performer. The Draupadi story is narrated by the *'kathak-thakuran'* supported by a chorus which acts both as a witness to, and a participant in, the unfolding drama. This shift in the tradition can be interpreted as deliberate. The tale of *'Nathabati Anathabat'* can only be narrated through the empathic vision of a woman-narrator. The induction of the indigenous element is again a self-reflexive strategy on the part of the dramatist: traditionally the *kathak-thakur* narrated epical, mythical and religious events, often scriptural and written in Sanskrit, therefore inaccessible to the predominantly female audience, thereby acting as a link between the sublime and the quotidian. In the subversion of this traditional paradigm, the new text subsumes the dialogic aspect of society with its class, ideological and hierarchical conflicts. That the narrative of the *kathak-thakuran* is valuable and valid is underscored by the way she is introduced to the reader/audience:

The girl is soft spoken, narrating the story with smile, and ad libs rhymes. But that does not muffle the sharpness of her approach. Indeed, there is a cutting edge to the way she speaks and moves; there is a conviction in what she says. This is what the 'Kathakthakuran' is like. (4)

The speaker begins with a play upon Kashiram Das's injunction of *'Mahabharata katha amrita saman'* in her insistence,

> The words of the Mahabharata
> Are ineffable like amrita
> In every age there unfold
> New meanings from the old. (6)

Mitra, in her 'literary archaeology', tries to unearth 'new meanings from the old'.

The narrator sets out to tell the story of 'a queen – yet not a queen. An empress – yet not an empress. Mistress of a kingdom. Yet a queen without a kingdom. . .' (6). The binaries along which Draupadi's character is constructed reveal the conflicts/contradictions central to her character and destiny. The *swayamvar* arranged by Drupad to marry off Draupadi to a 'true and tested warrior' is not in any way an exercise of free will, where the woman chooses her husband; rather, it is a camouflage for commoditisation where 'each thinks he will come, conquer, slip on the garland, grab the bride and drag her off with him' (8). Underlying the pomp and opulence of the *swayamvar sabha*, lurks the unsavoury truth that Draupadi will be offered to the highest bidder. The *swayamvar sabha* resembles an auction site, the 'prize', Draupadi, entering bashfully:

> Jewelled garland in her hands,
> Her head demurely bowed,
> Slowly to court the maiden goes,
> With solemn grace endowed;
> Her dazzling beauty glows,
> To the court the maiden goes,
> O to the court the maiden goes. (14)

Dhristyadyumna, Draupadi's brother, calls out to the assembled men in the tone of a peddler selling his wares: 'Come, honourable gentlemen, whichever high-born person can string this enormous bow and hit the target with five arrows through the aperture in the apparatus above... (14). Mitra subtly suggests the sexual predation of the assembled men towards Draupadi by comically presenting their haste and clamour to string the bow:

> There is a great scramble to grab the first chance. They all imagine, of course, that whoever gets to try first would shoot the arrows and make off with the maiden.... Remember Shalyaraj? You know the maternal uncle of Nakul and Sahadev. Surely he must be quite old eh? But his appetite hasn't ebbed! (14–15)

The 'sharing' of Draupadi by all the brothers, following the inviolable decree of mother Kunti exposes the female complicity in the perpetuation of patriarchal sexual dominance: 'And Kunti is wise. She knows that disputes arise mainly over property and over women. If her sons were to fall out with one another over a woman, how would they recover their lost kingdom...?' (23) The *kathak* raises a pertinent question: '... but no one even thought of asking Draupadi' (24). No one asks her when Yudhisthir stakes her in the gamble with the Kauravas. No one asks her, when she is dragged into the middle of the court and disrobed by the valiant men assembled in the royal court. But Draupadi asks an ethical question regarding the validity of the stake in which she is lost and won; Yudhisthir having lost himself already in the earlier stake has forfeited any right over Draupadi. But the *kathak* is quick to point out the irony: 'Gentlemen, could hair-splitting debates save Draupadi in this situation? What was needed to save her was anger. And arms [then ridiculing the role traditionally assigned to providence in saving Draupadi, she says] or Providence' (37).

The public disrobing of Draupadi assumes the signification of gang-rape, if not in praxis, but in essence: 'Dushasan approaches her from the left. But, draped in one piece of cloth, she is too embarrassed to get up quickly.... A woman in danger tries desperately to escape, but cannot.... It is said they laughed a lot' (38). She was subjected to further torments at the hands of Jayadrath and Kichak; she had to undergo the hardships of exile, yet she was always counselled to be calm, to forsake private anger for political expediency. The insult she suffered could not trigger *Dharmayuddha*; rather, Duryodhan's obduracy caused the war. Draupadi's aside reveals the moral vacuity of the war: 'If I forget the humiliation inflicted on me . . . will it usher a *Dharmarajya*, the rule of Virtue into this world? Can you promise that in the future no woman will ever be persecuted and demeaned like I was? Will my forgiveness usher in that heavenly state?' (60)

The irony inherent in Draupadi's destiny is insinuated by Vyasdev's description – *Nathabati Anathabat*, 'with lords but none a protector' (62). The irony is, however, differently conveyed in the play. Draupadi's plight is iteratively patterned as a counterpoint to her social identity as a daughter and wife of eminent men:

> Married to valiant lords,
> Yet none a protector,
> Such is the fate of
> Drupad's darling daughter;
> Unbelievable pain and bitterness. . . . (63)

The refrain underlines the undeniable reality that women have seldom been assigned subjectivity or agency; their identity has generally been derived from, or defined by, patriarchy. Mitra employs the same strategy of imaginative reconstruction in the denouement of the play as Karve does in *Yuganta*. Draupadi trudges along with the Pandavas to the gates of heaven, falls behind and fails to gain admittance. Dharmaraja Yudhisthir states the reason emphatically: 'For the sin of loving Arjun the most' (66). Though compelled into polygamy, Draupadi is expected to be equally loyal to her husbands. The same rule, however, does not apply to the 'valiant lords'. In her last moments, Draupadi ponders: '. . . What is love? Whom did Arjun love? There were so many women in his life – Ulipi, Chitrangada, Subhadra . . . Pramila. Which of them had he really loved? Had he ever loved any woman at all?' (67). Draupadi's suffering was real, that of flesh and blood, of life itself. Mitra says, 'Iravatididi has called it the suffering of an entire age. Draupadi endured the agony of a corrupt, decadent era' (64).

2

Fairy tales provide a repository of archetypal stories for recycling and revising, by different cultures and ages. The non-specific abstract contexts of fairy tales, the towers, castles and enchanted forests, give the impression of a never-land, which can be anytime, anywhere. However, the dark subtexts of fairy tales yield to the revisionist strategy of the later writer offering variations on forbidden or taboo subject matters such as incest, rape and familial violence. The reconfiguration and remaking of old tales into new ones, attempted by later authors, often reveal sexual undertones in tales which seem apparently to be tales of damsels in distress, beautiful princesses, brave and handsome princes, culminating, after various adventures, in happy endings. Fairy tales depict the inevitable process of growth and development since they predominantly deal with characters caught in the threshold between childhood and maturity, innocence and experience. They are an especially interesting and cogent area of analysis from a feminist perspective, since they tend to mould young girls' psyche with irrevocable consequences. The ideology and values that fairy tales reveal in the depiction of a 'perfect couple', the handsome prince and the beautiful princess, living a 'happily-ever-after' plot, can lead to the internalisation of a set of misleading patterns and structures by young girls.

Angela Carter's *The Bloody Chambers and Other Stories* (first published in 1979) retells the stories of Bluebeard, Snow White, Red Riding Hood and Puss and the Boots, and unearths different meanings in the process. It is interesting to note that Carter had translated Charles Perrault's tales a few years prior to her writing *The Bloody Chambers*. That perhaps provided her with clues regarding the embedded ambivalences and contradictions in these conventional tales. Carter's own definition of fairy tales is pertinent here:

> The chances are, the story was put together in the form we have it, more or less out of all sorts of bits of other stories long ago and far away and has been tinkered with, had bits added to it, lost other bits, got mixed with other stories, until our informant herself has tailored the story personally to suit an audience, or, simply, to suit herself. (Cavallaro 134)

The story of Little Red Riding Hood has been recycled, bits added and clipped, from the time it made its first appearance in the seventeenth century in the works of the French author Charles Perrault (1628–1703). It was a cautionary tale meant for young impressionable girls against strangers, here symbolised by the figure of the big bad wolf and the dark presence of the forest. The story is about a little girl who goes to meet her grandmother on the other side of the village across a forest, wearing a red hood. The wolf devours both the grandmother and the little girl at the end of the story, where the moral is explicit. There are dangers in society which not only threaten but may also consume and annihilate the young, respectable, well-bred young woman if she is not careful. The wolf signifies the perils of dishonour, indignity and rape that confront young girls who do not pay heed to the voices of caution. The ideology that is manifest in the tale is predicated upon the patriarchal stereotyping of the feminine as diffident and vulnerable; the ideal woman is expected to be chaste and aware of the pitfalls that await those who dare to be subversive.

Carter's 'The Company of Wolves' revisits the old tale from a new perspective. The wolf in the new text is 'carnivore incarnate and he's cunning as he is ferocious; once he's had a taste of flesh then nothing else will do' (139). The time of the year is not spring, but winter solstice, emblematic of a threshold which is reinforced by the girl in the story, who hovers between adolescence and maturity: 'She stands and moves within the invisible pentacle of her own virginity. She is an unbroken egg: she is a sealed vessel; she has inside her a magic space . . . she is a closed system; she does not know how to shiver' (143). The recalcitrance of the 'little' Red Riding Hood is evident as the author points out, 'She has her knife and she is afraid of nothing' (143). The wolf appears before her as a young man, with whom she strikes an immediate rapport, accepting the challenge of racing him to her grandmother's house. The prize promised is a kiss. The red hood that the girl wears gradually assumes a wider significance. It is a mark of difference; but scarlet is no longer the colour of shame, but of defiance and challenge against the internalised and indoctrinated structures of morality that is based on denial and repression. Red becomes symbolic of the instinctual and natural life.

The werewolf reaches the grandmother's house earlier than the young girl, dispenses with his human disguise and devours the grandmother. The god-fearing grandmother with the Bible at hand is symbolic of the rigid, orthodox and regressive religious and social structure; and her annihilation by the wolf is emblematic of the dismantling of this structure by anarchic and radical forces. Meanwhile, the girl reaches the cottage and discovers the duplicity of the wolf. But in contrast to the source text, the girl is not outwitted and consumed by the predator; she refuses to embrace the fate of passive victimhood. The archetypal catechism is reversed here: 'What big arms you have. All the better to hug you with. . . . What big teeth you have! . . . All the better to eat you with' (149). The threat is not met with terror by any wilting virgin, but with ridicule and aggression. 'The girl burst out laughing; she knew she was nobody's meat. She laughed at him full in the face, she ripped off his shirt for him and flung it into the fire, in the fiery wake of her own discarded clothing' (149). Even the terrible clattering of the grandmother's bones, symbolic of society's censure at her daring, cannot prevent her from taking the initiative in this game. The 'company of wolves' outside the cottage howls a 'prothalamion' (144), celebrating the 'savage marriage ceremony'; the forest sounds the Wagnerian *Liebestod* (144), thereby evoking the idea of 'love death' or consummation of love in death or after death. The new day after the momentous night is Christmas day, the werewolf's birthday. The choice of the day for the werewolf's birthday, which is mythically associated with the birth of the savior, is a deliberate subversion, a challenge to the paradigms of innocence and incorruptibility. Daybreak witnesses another upheaval and the author directs the reader's attention to the concluding scene: 'See! sweet and sound she sleeps in granny's bed, between the paws of the tender wolf' (150).

The old tale of caution is transmuted into an allegory of the sexual awakening of a pubescent young girl. She refuses to comply with the imposition of society's expectations of the untouched, unsullied virtuous maid. With this wilful coupling, the author liberates the character from the constraints of the stereotype. The girl is revealed to be in possession of the same ruthlessness and wiliness that enable her to mediate with the predator on her own terms.

★★★★

The significance and inevitability of feminist literary criticism as a mode of critical inquiry and interventionist strategy are now indisputably established in theoretical paradigms. Feminist literary criticism aims to plug the gaps and silences vis-à-vis the issues of female representation and agency in literature, while questioning the authenticity of traditional canon-formation. While Saoli Mitra's feminist rewriting of the *Mahabharata* questions the limited nature of the conventional reading of texts as well as the inequalities inherent in patriarchy, Angela Carter's reconfiguration of traditional fairy tales challenges the assumptions of male textuality. The tradition that was inaugurated with Virginia Woolf's *A Room of One's Own* (1929) has evolved to include such feminist literary critical studies as Patricia Meyer Spacks's *The Female Imagination: A Literary and Psychological Investigation of Women's Writing* (1972), Ellen Moers's *Literary Women: The Great Writers* (1976), Elaine Showalter's *A Literature of their Own: British Women Novelists from Bronte to Lessing* (1977), and Sandra Gilbert and Susan Gubar's *The Madwoman in the Attic* (1979). Feminist literary criticism, apart from re-evaluating women's experience and representation in literature both by male and female writers, reconsiders the implications of sexual difference and creativity. The insights of other theoretical frameworks such as Marxism, poststructuralism, psychoanalysis and postcolonialism have considerably shaped feminist literary criticism by providing pluralistic points of reference. The unpacking of the signifier 'woman', as constructed by patriarchy and manifest in overt and insidious sociocultural practices and contexts, emerges as a major trope in feminist literary criticism.

REFERENCES

Carter, Angela. *The Bloody Chamber and Other Stories*. New York: Penguin Books, 1979. Print.
Cavallaro, Dani. *The World of Angela Carter: A Critical Investigation*. North Carolina: McFarland and Company, 2011. Print.
Karve, Irawati. *Yuganta: The End of an Epoch*. New Delhi: Orient BlackSwan, 2007. Print.
Kristeva, Julia. *Desire in Language: A Semiotic Approach to Literature and Art*. Trans. Thomas Gora, Alice Jardine, and Leon S. Roudiez. Ed. Leon S. Roudiez. New York: Columbia UP, 1980. Print.
Mitra, Saoli. *Five Lords, Yet None a Protector and Timeless Tales: Two Plays*. Trans. Rita Datta. Kolkata: Stree, 2006. Print.
Wardle, Cathy Helen. *Beyond Ècriture Fèminine: Repetition and Transformation in the Prose Writing of Jeanne Hyvrard*. London: Modern Humanities Research Association, 2007. Print.

Glossary of Select Terms

Abjection: Julia Kristeva, in *Powers of Horror: An Essay on Abjection* (1982), argues that a subject, in order to enter the Symbolic order, needs to reject anything that endangers her/his autonomy and independence. The abject is associated with the unclean: food, vomit, bodily wastes, all reminders of the biological fallibility of the subject over which he/she has no control. The most notable of the abjected entity is the mother. To enter the Symbolic order, the child must renounce its connection with the mother; but it is a problematic process, so that the abject continues to haunt the subject.

Angel in the House: The idea was derived from Coventry Patmore's nineteenth-century poem, 'The Angel in the House', in which he presents an ideal of feminine virtues in the woman/wife modelled upon his wife Elizabeth. This Victorian image of an ideal woman/wife who is submissive, graceful and self-effacing is manifest in the poem: 'Man must be pleased, but him to please / Is woman's pleasure. . . .' This concept was critiqued by Virginia Woolf who argued in favour of 'killing' the 'angel of the house' by annihilating this internalised standard of desirable womanhood, for women to be truly liberated. In her essay 'The Angel in the House', Woolf exhorts women to break free of the mould of pure, innocent, angelic womanhood. In 'Three Guineas', she emphasised the necessity of killing 'the lady' even when 'the woman' still remained. Later feminists such as Ned Noddings and Charlotte Perkins Gilman were also dismissive of this model as infantile, weak and mindless.

Androcentrism: Derived from the Greek *'andro'* (meaning 'man'), androcentrism implies a male-centric worldview. Charlotte Perkins Gilman, in *The Man-Made World or Our Androcentric Culture* (1911), first introduced this term to describe the masculine practices predominant in society. Androcentrism privileged the masculine point of view as normative and denigrated the feminine point of view as the 'other'. Art, literature, educational policies, religion, politics, etc., explicitly advocate androcentrism, relegating women to an inferior position. The androcentric worldview upholds masculine traits, principles and values as superior and normative. This disadvantaged women, since they were considered to be deviants from the norm and were expected to be subordinate to androcentric ideology.

Androgyny: The term combines two Greek words *'andro'* and *'gyne'* meaning 'man' and 'woman' respectively. This concept represents an individual who possesses features of both masculinity and femininity. Virginia Woolf, in *A Room of One's Own*, introduces this idea into the feminist discourse. Following Samuel Taylor Coleridge's concept of an androgynous creative mind, Woolf challenges gender dichotomy, by insisting that bodies may be divided into two sexes but the mind can contain both masculine and feminine qualities. Woolf identifies this androgynous trait in writers such as Shakespeare, Keats, Sterne, Cowper, Lamb, Coleridge and Proust. She develops this idea of androgyny in her novel *Orlando*, in which the protagonist navigates time, first as a man and then as a woman. Carolyn Heilbrun, in *Toward a Recognition of Androgyny*, argues for a movement away from gender confinements towards a liberating ideal of androgyny. This concept of androgyny can also be viewed as the source of the postmodern tendency of interpreting performativity of gender in cross-dressing and masquerading.

Antifeminism: Antifeminism is simply defined as the opposition to feminism. Antifeminists advocate subordinate roles for women and attack any attempts towards granting gender equality. Susan Faludi's *Backlash: The Undeclared War against American Women* depicts the antifeminist propaganda that maligns the feminist efforts towards seeking liberty and empowerment in a discriminatory society. Antifeminists also include women who claim that domestic and conventional roles are best suited to women. Antifeminists attack feminists by invoking myths about women's inferiority. Antifeminism has taken different forms and attitudes across time. In the nineteenth century, antifeminists opposed the suffrage movement and the efforts of women directed towards accessing higher education. Subsequently, they opposed such legislative movements as the Equal Rights Amendment. In extreme situations, antifeminism can take violent forms as in the massacre of female engineering students in the University of Montreal in 1989.

Binary Oppositions: The term refers to the pairs of opposites predominant in language and culture since the Enlightenment. Binary opposites include male/female, white/black, reason/emotion, active/passive, subject/object, presence/absence and self/other. French theorist Jacques Derrida argues that epistemology is constructed around this system of binaries wherein one component of the pair is dominant over the other. For example, in the male-female dyad, the masculine is privileged over the feminine. Another important aspect of this structure is the dependence of one category's dominance on the other. The dominance of the privileged component of the pair is compromised in the absence of the 'other'. Thus, the dominant category needs the subordinate element to reinforce its own superiority. Derrida's idea of binary opposition greatly influenced feminist theorists such as Hélène Cixous. Feminists challenge binary oppositions because they imply the primacy of one category over the other.

Base/Superstructure: In Marxist theory, base-superstructure signifies the relationship between the modes of production and the structure of power in society. The base is the economic system determined by modes of production while the superstructure is the religious, political and legal institutions by which ideology is produced and propagated. The relationship between the base and the superstructure is a complex one, which determines class power. For Marx, the superstructure is generally dependent on the modes of production predominant in a given time. Changes in the base are determined by the changes in the modes of production in a society. The historically determined changes in a society's base will, in turn, change the ideological superstructure. In feminist theory, base-superstructure is viewed in relation to the ways in which gender is constructed and influenced.

Consciousness-raising (groups): These were the groups formed during the second-wave feminism in the 1970s that encouraged women to talk about their personal experiences including the hitherto forbidden or taboo subjects such as sexuality, abortion and abuse. 'Consciousness-raising' validated the personal life by underscoring the authenticity of women's expression of their lived experiences. This exercise was intended to raise the awareness of the group in general, and the individual recounting her experiences, in particular. This became a mass organising tool to understand the ways of oppression and to build a movement against them. This was a programme undertaken by the New York Radical Women group in 1968. Some radical actions were also triggered by the awareness generated by the consciousness-raising sessions. The strength of the programme lay in its egalitarian approach – anyone could do it.

Difference Feminism: Difference feminism is associated with Carol Gilligan, Hélène Cixous and Luce Irigaray. They argue in favour of acknowledging and celebrating the differences between men and women, rather than considering women as 'lack'. Liberal feminists advocated equal rights and status for women, thereby privileging the ideals of rationality and humanism. Difference feminists, on the other hand, seek alternative structures and discourses valorising the 'differences' between men and women, central among them being the child-bearing ability of women. Difference feminists insist that women are 'naturally' more caring, compassionate and generous than men. Some feminist critics, however, find difference feminism essentialist and as a movement that may lead to an acceptance of the restrictive roles ascribed to women. Other feminists of difference, such as Irigaray and Cixous, undertake an analysis of the processes by which gender is constructed. Instead of celebrating the 'differences' or rejecting them altogether, they seek to understand these 'differences' as sites of repression and resistance.

Enlightenment: The Enlightenment was an age of heightened philosophical and intellectual movement between 1688 and 1789, when the French Revolution began. The principles guiding Enlightenment philosophy were rationality, reason, justice and the spirit of inquiry. Philosophers such as John Locke rejected the unquestioning allegiance to traditions. Rousseau's *Social Contract* (1762) put forward the ideas of civil liberty, thereby providing impetus to the American War of Independence and the French Revolution. Enlightenment philosophy promotes universal education, political freedom and social equality, and produces rationality, which is necessary to critique the dominant discourses. Enlightenment ideals influenced and inspired the feminist aspirations of equality and justice. Mary Wollstonecraft, Olympe de Gouges and John Stuart Mill applied Enlightenment ideals in formulating feminist principles.

Essentialism: Essentialism in philosophy is understood as 'whatness' or the true essence of things. In feminist theory, anti-racist theory and gay/lesbian theory, the term 'essentialism' – like the terms biologism, naturalism and universalism – is used as a pejorative term because it classified gender, race or sexuality in terms of biological determinism. Essentialism overlooks the differences among women caused by differences of race, gender and sexuality, and tends to map a pattern of common oppression upon all women. Essentialism includes the tendency of upholding gender stereotypes as well as Radical feminists' attempts at creating a separate woman's culture. Cultural feminists have also been accused of being essentialists for emphasising women's capacity for care and nurturance. Gynocritics and French feminists were also dubbed as essentialists due to their assertion of a distinct female language and literary tradition. Thinkers such as Henry Louis Gates Junior and Judith Butler have revised the categories of race, sex and gender from an anti-essentialist perspective.

Ethics of Care: Ethics of care implies that there is a moral significance in the elements of relationships in human life. This moral theory is attributed to Carol Gilligan (*A Different View*) and Ned Noddings. Feminists often condemn care-based ethics for perpetuating essentialist stereotypes, but care-focused feminism privileges the ethics of care over the ethics of justice as the qualities which are exclusive to women. They need to be championed as strengths and not denigrated as weakness.

Fetishism: Fetishism is a term used in the Western traditions of psychology, aesthetics and economics. Marx and Freud invested fetishism with economic and psychological connotations. 'Fetishism of commodities', in Marxian parlance, signifies the process by which the workers are alienated from their produce, when commodities begin to take precedence over people. Fetishism in Freudian analysis is primarily a male condition in which the young boy substitutes the 'absent' penis of the mother with its approximations in an inanimate object, to avert the fear of castration. In feminist theory, fetishism is used to analyse the representation of women in literature. Critics have located portrayals of women as fetishised objects in literature. In visual arts, especially in films, women are often fetishised presences. Laura Mulvey calls it 'fetishistic scopophilia'. The fetishised, eroticised image of the woman is a reassuring presence because it can be controlled and fixed by the male gaze; on the other hand, the same object also holds the viewer in an 'erotic rapport'. Fetishism is also used as an important tool by feminist theorists to dismantle the hierarchy of great books or classics by denying them the possibility of possessing any inherent mystical quality.

Gaze: The 'gaze' represents the ways of seeing or looking that produces and circulates discourses of power. Michel Foucault refers to the medical gaze, while Jacques Lacan describes the role of gaze in the mirror stage of the development of human psyche. Cornel West provides the concept of 'normative gaze' by which he implies the Euro-centric gaze that provides a hegemonic perspective for analysing other racial identities. In feminist theory, the idea of gaze has been specifically disseminated in relation to visual cultures. Laura Mulvey, in her 1975 essay 'Visual Pleasure and Narrative Cinema', provides the concept of the 'male gaze', the fundamentally heterosexual male perspective of viewing the narrative of cinema. This idea offers insights into how men look at women, how women look at other women and how women look at themselves. In Mulvey's analysis, women are objectified by the 'male gaze' of the audience and are denied agency. Women among the audience also identify with this heterosexual male perspective to experience the narrative.

Gender: 'Gender' was initially used synonymously with 'women' and 'sexual differences'. Since the 1980s gender has become a more complex term of analysis. It implies knowledge of sexual difference as well as those socialisation processes by which individuals construct themselves as gendered beings. Gender is thus no longer a biological category but a cultural category influencing varied other discourses of philosophy, history, science, anthropology, psychology, etc. The term has special implications in feminist theory. Till the 1970s the terms 'gender' and 'sex' were used interchangeably. The analyses and theories of cultural feminists, gynocritics, French feminists and postmodern feminists point out that 'gender' is the meaning that culture and socialisation practices ascribe to biological differences. It constitutes a set of behaviours that is learned and performed.

Gynesis: 'Gynesis' is a term coined by Alice Jardine in *Gynesis: Configuration of Woman and Modernity* (1985), to signify the emergence of new concepts in Western thought which are gendered or feminine, causing disruptions in language and syntax and thereby challenging patriarchy. Jardine's concept of gynesis signifies the intersection of the French poststructuralist and feminist thought with the American literary tradition. Etymologically, gynesis implies 'woman-process' or 'putting into the discourse of woman'. Postmodern theorists have reinterpreted Western texts to identify sites where the text is disrupted by the sudden appearance of a woman who was hitherto silent or absent. Jardine terms this 'gynesis' or the production of 'feminine' texts in which 'killing of the father' is enacted by the disruption of language and narrative. Jardine argues that in American fiction, gynesis operates not at the level of language and syntax, but at the level of representation. Jardine finds 'gynesis' operative in the works of Jacques Derrida, Jacques Lacan and Gilles Deleuze.

Hysteria: 'Hysteria' is derived from the Greek word for 'womb', signifying mental disorders associated with women. There are references to hysterical, morbid mental states in Egyptian and Greek myths and legends, which are all related to the displacement of the uterus or the 'wandering womb'. Freud uses the Platonic idea of women's mental anguish caused by the distress of their uterus in his analysis of hysteria. In his first theory of hysteria, Freud states that hysteria is a delayed reaction of the repressed psyche to childhood abuse, thereby pinning the responsibility on the father. He later altered his theory to redefine hysteria as a delayed response to infantile sexual fantasies from a mature sexual perspective. In this theory, Freud displaces the guilt from the father to the child. In the 1933 essay 'Femininity', Freud finds in hysteria an expression of guilt from Oedipus Complex triggered by the contact with the body of the mother (or the nursemaid). The responsibility was now assigned to the mother. Feminist theory has received Freud's theories of hysteria with a great deal of contention, so that hysteria as a term has undergone revisions from being a pejorative term to an ambivalent and complex category. Feminist critics such as Elaine Showalter and Mary Jacobus exploded the myth of female hysteria and presented studies in male hysteria. Feminists find in hysteria a feminine proto-language which challenges patriarchy.

Identity Politics: It is a politics based on personal identity. Social and cultural upheavals in the 1960s and 70s raised questions regarding the representation of class interests, ethnicity, sexuality and ability. For the marginalised or excluded sections of society, identity politics – not organised around shared belief systems or party affiliations – became an important tool for resistance and challenge. Identity politics is of central concern to feminist critics. Feminism has the difficult task of situating identity politics without caving in to reductive essentialism. Identity politics, for feminists, aims to challenge the social constructions by which women are discriminated against, without complying with sexist views, so that the analysis of concepts such as 'maternal thinking', 'ècriture fèminine' or 'ethics of care' are imbricated in the ambivalent discourse of identity politics as well as essentialism. Some feminists argue that feminist thought should move beyond identity politics; but it is undeniable that the sex-gender dichotomy guides and determines feminist theory to a considerable degree.

Jouissance: In French *'jouissance'* means pleasure of an orgasmic nature. Feminist theorists find in *jouissance* a reflection of feminine pleasure and the potential to disrupt the phallogocentric discourse. *Jouissance* refers to women's physical and bodily pleasures without the intrusion of patriarchal norms. Roland Barthes, in *The Pleasure of the Text*, refers to the radical and disruptive *jouissance* as distinctive from the staid, manageable 'pleasure' derived from the text. Feminist theorists have employed this disruptive ideology of *jouissance* to present the possibility of female creative power and the ability to move beyond the ordinary realm of experience to an unbounded fluid state of being. This paradigm of female abundance of pleasure challenges restrictive patriarchal ideology. Luce Irigaray, Hélène Cixous and Julia Kristeva have explored the possibilities of female *jouissance* as a radical creative agency.

Masquerade: 'Masquerade' means disguise, but is assigned several symbolic meanings. Masquerade is treated as a carnivalesque tool to subvert the normative and to ironically comment on it. It can also provide clues to the ways in which identities/subjectivities are constructed. Joan Riverie finds in masquerade a conventional disguise of femininity that a woman assumes to mediate a predominantly patriarchal culture. In feminist literary criticism, the topos of masquerade is used both as a process by which women internalise the standards of femininity and also as a possibility of constructing an alternative female identity. Masquerade, in feminist theory, is presented as a strategy to conceal 'lack'. Riverie, in 'Womanliness as a Masquerade', argues that successful women, especially those engaged in intellectual pursuits, put on the masquerade of womanliness to diffuse their anxiety of transgression. The concept of masquerade has been taken up by feminist queer theorists to theorise the ways of constructing gender. Judith Butler, in *Gender Trouble*, argues that gender is 'performative', thereby revising the sex-gender dichotomy.

Masculinity: There has been a recent upsurge in the complex cultural construction around the idea of masculinity. Masculinity has been considered as 'normative' and masculine qualities such as courage, authority, independence, vigour and rationality have been upheld as valuable ideals. The 'feminine' is defined in relation (often contrapuntal) to these ideas of masculinity. But masculinity as a concept is no longer a stable category; like femininity, it is also inflected with contradictions and anxieties.

Marginality: In feminist theory, the term 'marginality' implies exclusion based on issues of race, class, gender, ethnicity or sexuality. It is assumed that groups with less power than the dominant group are left out from the precincts of the literary canon. Women are included in such groups. The term has been extended to apply to women of different races and classes who do not receive recognition unlike the more privileged among them. Barbara Smith, Cherrie Moraga and Gloria Anzaldúa have highlighted the marginality experienced by Third World women and women of colour. Theorists such as Gayatri Chakravorty Spivak have underscored the overlapping nature of the 'centre' and the 'margin', which necessitates a reviewing of the categories of 'margin' and 'marginality'. The idea of marginality is, however, crucial in feminism.

Matrocentric: 'Matrocentric' means 'centred on the mother'. In matrocentric societies mothers are valued and invested with socio-economic authority. In feminist theory, the term implies a rerouting of feminism in search of the foremothers. In feminist psychoanalysis, 'matrocentric' describes the bond between the mother and child in the pre-Oedipal or Semiotic stage which the adult daughter attempts to duplicate later. The French feminists especially assert the importance of matrocentricity in the construction of subjectivity and in creative expression.

Oedipus Complex: In Freudian psychoanalysis, the third/phallic stage in the psycho-sexual development of a child is distinguished by the Oedipus complex. In the Oedipal stage, the little boy sexually desires his mother and suffers from jealousy and murderous instincts towards the father. The Oedipus complex is subsequently moderated by another emotion, the fear of castration. This leads the little boy to identify with the authority of the father and move beyond his autoeroticism. The sexual desire that he felt for his mother is gradually replaced by his desire for other women. This sublimation of sexual desire ensures him access to the adult world though this transference is fraught with several anxieties and contradictions.

Other: The 'other' implies sexual and racial difference in binary structures (self-other). Traditionally, the masculine 'self' is constituted as the normative ideal, the 'other'/feminine principle is constructed in terms of 'lack'. Feminist theorists have revealed that Western philosophy has always represented women in a negative way in order to establish male supremacy. Otherness is also present in the conceptualisations of race. White hegemonic principles relegate all other racial identities to the location of the 'other'. Poststructuralist and postcolonial theories have complicated the concept of the 'other'. Gayatri Chakravorty Spivak locates the Third World woman in the location of the 'other'. Chandra Talpade Mohanty further complicates the category of the 'woman' as the 'other' into the material reality of 'women', in which the concept of 'otherness' is problematised by its possible diversity. The figure of the 'other', hitherto silenced and marginalised, in recent times is found to speak back and speak as themselves, thereby claiming agency and disrupting the hegemonic discourse.

Patriarchy: 'Patriarchy' literally means 'the rule of the father'. Culturally, patriarchy implies dominance of men over women. It is directed towards the oppression of women in all spheres of political, social and economic structures. Feminists have interpreted patriarchy variously. Radical feminists found patriarchy operating through sexual control and sexual stereotyping, putting women in subservient, diffident roles. Marxist feminism analyses patriarchy from the perspective of sexual division of labour perpetuated in the class system. Poststructuralist feminists view patriarchy in the use of phallogocentric language that reinforces gender stereotypes demeaning women. The role of man is primary in social organisations in patriarchy; the father being the head of the domestic sphere, he is the dominant figure of authority over women and children. Patriarchy privileges men and its continuation depends on female subordination. Women's access to resources, power and position is denied by patriarchal ideology, which inferiorises women. Feminist theory found patriarchy to be an unjust and unequal social system.

Penis Envy: In 'Infantile Genital Organization of the Libido', Freud presents a different explanation of the castration complex for the girl child (from the Oedipal complex and the fear of castration of boys). Freud argues that women suffer from a repressed desire to possess the phallus. As a little girl, she immediately understands her lack, blames her mother for her deficiency and in her fear of being castrated, she develops 'penis envy'. Feminist theory has berated Freudian assumptions of penis envy. Kate Millet, Mary Jacobus and Sarah Kofman find in Freud's theory of 'penis envy', the perpetuation of male prejudices and biases directed at segregating and belittling women.

Phallocentrism: 'Phallocentrism' literally means 'centring around the phallus'. Psychoanalytic theory, especially the Lacanian model, is found to be phallocentric in its insistence on the castration complex, and desire from the male perspective. Female sexuality is either ignored or represented negatively by male psychoanalysts. French feminists such as Luce Irigaray and Hélène Cixous offer alternative discourses to phallocentrism. The first critique of phallocentrism came from inside psychoanalysis, from analysts such as Melanie Klein, Ernest Jones and Karen Horney.

Phallogocentrism: 'Phallogocentrism' is a combination of phallocentrism (centring on the phallus) and logocentrism (word-centred). Phallogocentrism implies a phallus-centric thought process and language use. Phallocentric language is linear, structured, decisive and masculinist. The phallus is the representative of the norm and standard by which all else is defined. Luce Irigaray, Hélène Cixous and Monique Wittig challenge phallogocentrism that privileges the masculine order. Feminist critiques of phallogocentrism offer *'jouissance'* as its alternative.

Female bodily experiences, and libidinal pleasure, challenge the phallic order. The feminine way of speaking and writing, that is fluid and fragmented, challenges and subverts the structured linearity of phallogocentric language.

Voyeurism: 'Voyeurism' literally means 'to see'. In feminist theory, voyeurism/scopophilia denotes the masculine controlling gaze fixing a female subject, intruding upon boundaries and rendering her into an erotic/sexual entity. Laura Mulvey finds, in films, the eye of the camera and the audience deriving voyeuristic pleasure from the female object of desire on the screen.

Womanism: A term coined by Alice Walker in her essay 'In Search of Our Mothers' Gardens: Womanist Prose', 'Womanism' as a concept challenges the universalist assumptions of white feminism and dismisses separatist ideologies. It is an inclusive philosophy which acknowledges the importance of black men in the lives of black women. It is a woman-centred vision of liberation and engagement, resisting oppressive agencies. Walker defines a Womanist as 'a black feminist or feminist of color . . . who loves other women, sexually and/or non-sexually . . . committed to the survival and wholeness of an entire people, male and female.' Womanism celebrates the sexuality and strength of black women, recognising the fact that they are survivors of violence and abuse.

Suggested Reading

Abel, Elizabeth, Barbara Christian, and Helene Moglen, eds. *Female Subjects in Black and White: Race, Psychoanalysis, Feminism*. Berkeley: U of California P, 1997. Print.

Ahmed, Sara. *Differences that Matter: Feminist Theory and Postmodernism*. Cambridge: Cambridge UP, 2004. Print.

Butler, Judith. *Gender Trouble: Feminism and the Subversion of Identity*. New York and London: Routledge, 1990. Print.

Brennen, Teresa, ed. *Between Feminism and Psychoanalysis*. London and New York: Routledge, 1992. Print.

Brooks, Ann. *Postfeminisms: Feminism, Cultural Theory and Cultural Forms*. New York: Routledge, 1997. Print.

Campbell, Jan. *Arguing with the Phallus, Feminist, Queer and Postcolonial Theory: A Psychoanalytic Contribution*. London: Zed Books, 2000. Print.

Cavallaro, Dani. *French Feminist Theory: An Introduction*. London and New York: Continuum, 2003. Print.

de Beauvoir, Simone. *The Second Sex*. Trans. H. M. Parshley. New York: Vintage, 1989. Print.

Dicker, Rory C. *A History of U.S. Feminisms*. Berkeley: Seal Press, 2008. Print.

Eagleton, Mary, ed. *A Concise Companion to Feminist Theory*. Oxford: Blackwell, 2003. Print.

Elam, Diane. *Feminism and Deconstruction*. London: Routledge, 1994. Print.

Fernald, Anne E. *Virginia Woolf: Feminism and the Reader*. New York: Palgrave Macmillan, 2006. Print.

Fuss, Diana, ed. *Inside/Out: Lesbian Theories, Gay Theories*. New York and London: Routledge, 1991. Print.

Gilbert, Sandra M., and Susan Gubar. *No Man's Land: The Place of the Woman Writer in the Twentieth Century*. New Haven: Yale UP, 1988. Print.

Gillis, Stacy, Gillian Howies, and Rebecca Munford. *Third Wave Feminism: A Critical Exploration*. New York: Palgrave Macmillan, 2004. Print.

Grewal, Inderpal, and Caren Kaplan, eds. *Scattered Hegemonies: Postmodernity and Transnational Feminist Practices*. Minneapolis: U of Minnesota P, 1994. Print.

Hannam, June. *Feminism*. Harlow: Pearson Education Limited, 2007. Print.

Hurley, Jennifer A. *Feminism: Opposing Viewpoints*. California: Greenhaven Press, 2001. Print.

Jackson, Stevi, and Jackie Jones. *Contemporary Feminist Theories*. Edinburgh: Edinburgh UP, 1998. Print.

Kristeva, Julia. *Desire in Language: A Semiotic Approach to Literature and Art*. Ed. Leon S. Roudiez. New York: Columbia UP, 1980. Print.

Minh-ha, Trinh T. *Woman, Native, Other: Writing Postcoloniality and Feminism*. Bloomington: Indiana UP, 1989. Print.

Mohanty, Chandra Talpade, Ann Russo, and Lourdes Torres, eds. *Third World Women and the Politics of Feminism*. Bloomington: Indiana UP, 1991. Print.

Nicholson, Linda, ed. *Feminism/Postmodernisms*. New York: Routledge, 1990. Print.

Nye, Andrea. *Feminism and Modern Philosophy: An Introduction*. New York: Routledge, 2004. Print.

Osborne, Susan. *Feminism*. Harpenden: Pocket Essentials, 2001. Print.

Rhodes, Jacqueline. *Radical Feminism, Writing and Critical Agency: From Manifesto to Modem*. Albany: State U of New York P, 2005. Print.

Rooney, Ellen, ed. *The Cambridge Companion to Feminist Literary Theory*. Cambridge: Cambridge UP, 2006. Print.

Sandoval, Chela. *Methodology of the Oppressed*. Minneapolis: U of Minnesota P, 2000. Print.

Sedgwick, Eve Kosofsky. *Epistemology of the Closet*. London: Penguin, 1994. Print.

Sharpe, Jenny. *Allegories of Empire: The Figure of the Woman in the Colonial Text*. Minneapolis: U of Minnesota P, 1993. Print.

Spivak, Gayatri Chakravorty. *In Other Worlds: Essays in Cultural Politics*. New York: Methuen, 1987. Print.

Tong, Rosemarie. *Feminist Thought*. Colorado: Westview Press, 2009. Print.

Wallace, Elizabeth Kowaleski, ed. *Encyclopedia of Feminist Literary Theory*. New York: Routledge, 2009. Print.

Walters, Margaret. *Feminism: A Very Short Introduction*. New York: Oxford UP, 2005. Print.

Literary Contexts recognises that literature is always rooted in its social milieu and that we need to study literary cultures in all their complexity and connections. It offers the thrill of locating a text within its context and seeing a context reflected in a literary/cultural text.

Each of the books in the series offers students of English and other literatures concise, informative insights into the history of ideas embodied in literary texts, authors and movements. Organised around themes and ideas with extensive examples from literary and cultural texts, the books enable students to understand how the "literary" takes shape in an intellectual milieu and discover manifestations of abstract ideas in literary texts. Written by scholar-teachers who have taught and researched literature for several years, each volume in the series is a stand-alone reference book for students and teachers alike.

Series Editor
Pramod K. Nayar teaches at the Department of English, The University of Hyderabad. His most recent books include *The Transnational in English Literature: Shakespeare to the Modern* (2015), *Citizenship and Identity in the Age of Surveillance* (2015), *The Postcolonial Studies Dictionary* (2015) and *Postcolonial Studies: An Anthology* (2015). His forthcoming work includes a book on the Indian graphic novel.

Titles in the Series
Shakespeare   Postcolonial Literatures
American Literature   Victorian Literature
Modern English Literature   Postmodern Literatures
Eighteenth-century English Literature

CRITICAL EDITIONS

Co-published by

The English and Foreign Languages University, Hyderabad

Orient BlackSwan

Series Editors
T. Sriraman, Lakshmi Chandra and Lavanya Kolluri
EFL-U, Hyderabad

About the series: *Critical Editions* is a series jointly published by the English and Foreign Languages University and Orient BlackSwan with the aim of bringing literary texts closer to students of both undergraduate and postgraduate levels. Each edition not only explores the structure and texture of the text chosen but also places it in its literary and cultural context. These editions are introduced and edited by reputed academic experts and are supported by their experience of teaching and interacting with students over a number of years.

Published

English Poetry 1660–1780: An Anthology.
Edited by Pramod K. Nayar, Department of English, University of Hyderabad

Robinson Crusoe by Daniel Defoe
Edited by Pramod K. Nayar, Department of English, University of Hyderabad

Emma by Jane Austen
Edited by Sunita Mishra, Centre for English Language Studies, University of Hyderabad

Wuthering Heights by Emily Brontë
Edited by Sunita Mishra, Centre for English Language Studies, University of Hyderabad

Gulliver's Travels by Jonathan Swift
Edited by Pramod K. Nayar, Department of English, University of Hyderabad

Modern English Poetry: A Selection
Edited by Mohan G. Ramanan, Department of English, University of Hyderabad

Tess of the d'Urbervilles by Thomas Hardy
Edited by John Varghese, The English and Foreign Languages University (EFL-U)